Otto Eduard Lessing

Masters in Modern German Literature

———

Detlev von Liliencron

Masters in Modern German Literature

by

Otto Eduard Lessing

University of Illinois

Mit einem Bildnis von Detlev von Liliencron

Essay Index Reprint Series

BOOKS FOR LIBRARIES PRESS, INC.
FREEPORT, NEW YORK

Originally published by:
Verlag von Carl Reissner

First published 1912
Reprinted 1967

PRINTED IN THE UNITED STATES OF AMERICA

Dem Bahnbrecher deutscher Kultur
in Amerika:

Kuno Francke

Contents:

I.

Modern Literature in Germany

The word m o d e r n has a specific meaning in the German art and literature of the last generation. There were and there still are people who associate with it an absurdly tasteless kind of furniture and architecture; or "ugly" pictures of cabbage-fields and cow-barns, or immoral and degenerately pessimistic poems, novels, dramas. On the other hand there are people for whom the same word means a wealth of radiant light and color, of grand, and delicate, and joyous beauty; of an art and literature, simple, natural, and true in its mode of expression, dignified and noble in its effect, bravely affirmative in its philosophy. Schiller was "modern", when he published T h e R o b b e r s and was condemned as a maniac by some, hailed as a German Shakespeare by others. Heinrich von Kleist was "modern", when Goethe timidly turned away from him and Tieck recognized his genius. And so forth to Hebbel and Wagner and Ibsen and Boecklin and Hugo Wolf and Whistler until this very day. The word m o d e r n , just as the word romantic, means everything and nothing and was, like this, used as a program.

In 1886 a group of young writers in Berlin made it the war-cry against pseudo-romantic and pseudo-classic convention, against Paul Heyse's cult of superficial beauty, against Spielhagen's rationalistic shallowness, against Felix Dahn's ultra-patriotic bombast, against the archaic shampoetry of Julius Wolff and Georg Ebers. The muse of the new storm and stress, as one of its early spokesmen put it, is "a modern, i. e. a knowing and yet pure woman, in the attitude of advance, inspiring and uplifting mankind by her perfection of all earthly beauty — the symbol of the new art: M o d e r n i s m." In other words, the aim of art is beauty founded upon truth; it is the expression of the vital forces in the evolution of the race. Such definitions as this did not essentially differ from Goethe's or Schiller's; and the public might have rested assured that the world's peace was to remain undisturbed by the theories of the Berlin literati.

However, M o d e r n i s m was quite independent of literary coteries. It was, so it seemed to conservative citizens, a very shrewdly organized conspiracy against state, church, morals, and esthetic sense of polite society. Was it not also called "Naturalism" being most closely connected with that international nihilism the head-quarters of which lay somewhere in St. Petersburg, or in Babylon Paris, or in the Scandinavian North? Either Tolstoy, or Zola, or Ibsen, or some other of those suspicious foreigners had invented that dangerous new thing which threatened to undermine civilization. To read Zola or Tolstoy was high-treason, and whoever found in Ibsen's plays a stirring call to self-criticism and rigorous purity of morals was counted among the hopelessly degenerate. In an hysterical opposition to the new movement the good citizens with increased

zeal turned to the gilt-edged banalities and sweet-sixteen
erotica of those very favorites of fashion who disgusted the
young champions for truth and power.

After Germany had victoriously emerged from one of
the greatest and bloodiest wars of the world's history, its
"intellectual" public contented itself with a literature as
weakly, untrue, and lifeless as the pastoral poetry of
Martin Opitz and his school. While Germany's economic
condition underwent the radical transformation from an
agricultural to an industrial country, and the breach
between capitalism and labor-proletariat seemed to en-
danger the existence of the newly founded empire; while
natural sciences and philosophy, with an unheard-of audacity, penetrated into the secrets of creation striving to
reform religion and ethics on the basis of startling discoveries; while, in short, a revolution was taking place
more intensive and extensive than the revolution of 1789 —
amidst these momentous events the German philistines
worshipped the shallowest of their day as the nation's
representative authors.

Indeed — and here the philistines were right — there
was going on a revolution. Only it was not the "modern"
literature that caused it, but the progress of science and the
political, social, and economic developments. Germany
after 1870, compared to Germany of 1850, was a strangely
interesting, complex, and problematical phenomenon. But
the public was reluctant to face the new era openly. The
ostrich method of hiding in the bush gave too much com-
fort not to he applied. Neither in literature nor in art

people wished to be reminded of the fact that the age of Bismarck and Bebel was different from the age of Metternich, that the time of the "German Michael's" lazy drowsiness had passed. Literature and art were to follow the old ruts of conventionality, as if nothing had happened.

But art and literature, like everything else in this world of ours, are the result of general laws. They do not serve the subjective arbitrariness of individuals but fulfill their duty of giving expression to their respective periods. It is, therefore, absurd and useless to oppose N a t u r a - l i s m or M o d e r n i s m with hostile contempt. We must learn to know it as an historical fact and to appreciate its works as we appreciate the works of any other art-movement: romanesque, gothic, renaissance, and so forth. Taking, for the present, M o d e r n i s m and N a t u r a l - i s m as identical terms — what then, we ask, does "Naturalism" mean? Naturalism as a philosophical system believes in the reality and objective value of what to our senses appears as nature. Naturalism as an artistic tendency is based upon such belief and attempts to grasp the life ("nature") of a given time in its essential meaning. It attempts to be absolutely true to nature. It attempts to cast into the forms of art as much as possible of nature's inexhaustible treasures. Naturalism has no dogmatic creed of beauty. It does not recognize any convention. It does not consider "beauty" an a-priori-ideal, but a reality springing forth ever anew from the ever changing harmony of form and content. Since form and content determine each other mutually, every new content must have a rela-

tively new form, otherwise the essence and substance of
the content, (truth, nature), cannot be expressed, that is
to say: the result is not a work of art, is not that highest
kind of beauty which is identical with truth.

This modern "return to nature" has often been likened
to eighteenth century Rousseauism. Indeed there was the
protest against convention, the cry for originality as during
the "storm and stress". But the modern conception of
nature had nothing at all to do with Rousseau's sentimental
idea of retrogression into primitive barbarism. Modern
naturalism included all the complexities of metropolitan
cities, of commercial and social organizations, and so forth;
it discovered civilization in its widest sense as a part of
human life, of nature. The democratic spirit of the
eighteenth century had admitted the third estate, the
citizen-class, to its place in art. Naturalism not only
admitted the fourth estate, the proletariat, but expanded
the sphere of art beyond all limits whatsoever, true to
Goethe's word that any part of reality might be made the
subject of art. Naturalism is as progressively universal
as Friedrich Schlegel's romanticism.

To be sure, the discovery of new material was one
thing, the perfection of form another. Men like M i c h a e l
G e o r g C o n r a d and M a x K r e t z e r reached into
the fulness of life about them, finding it all interesting.
But their modes of expression were borrowed from abroad.
What they produced were monstrosities of formlessness
that ill compared with the smooth verses of Julius Wolff
or with the aristocratic parlorscenes of Paul Heyse. There

were writers who, in their efforts to avoid the suspicion
of catering to any traditional sense of beauty, went so far
as to make a melancholy specialty of representing the
misery of the proletariat, the vice in the slums of big cities,
the slavery in mining or manufacturing concerns.   There
were painters who year after year exhibited canvasses of
cabbage-fields, hay-stacks, and cow-barns.   Such experiments — technically very valuable as they might be —, such
exaggerations were an easy prey for the philistine's scorn;
they were, in their brutal crassness, apt to spoil both moral
and esthetic sense of the immature.   That was one phase
of "naturalism".

But is there any art-movement without its undesirable
and transient extremes?   Do we judge Shakespeare by
Titus Andronicus or Schiller by The Robbers?
Truth with genuine naturalism did not mean rudeness or
externalism but differentiation, harmony of style, intern-
alism. This may best be exemplified by works of pictorial
art.   In the eighties there were no religious paintings more
popular than Plockhorst's scenes from the life of Jesus.
They invariably showed an exceptionally handsome some-
body, dressed in blue and red broadcloth, theatrically
posed, neither a human being nor a God.   Nor did the
paintings as such do justice to the artiste problems involved.   The "naturalist" Fritz von Uhde came with his
conception of The Saviour, startled the public at first,
finally drew it away from those conventional nothings.
Uhde's Jesus appeared in all his simplicity and humility, a

real Son of Man, a real Saviour who gathered about him the children and the weary and sorrowful: and yet a real Son of God of purest spirituality, of divine dignity. And these unassuming pictures were indeed p a i n t e d , showing the finest color gradations and effects of air and light; all from within, from the very essence of the subject-matter; no trace of external decoration. Another example from the opposite point of view: war. Compare Franz Stuck's well-known painting of that name with its many allegorical predecessors, like Dürer's or Cornelius' A p o - c a l y p t a n R i d e r s ,   or Kaulbach's B a t t l e w i t h t h e H u n s , or Böcklin's W a r . These are phantoms, suspended in the air, entirely failing of their mission which evidently is to inspire awe and terror. Inspecting them we involuntarily call for a commentary to tell us what we are supposed to feel. Now Stuck: He does not give an abstract allegory but the thing itself concretely symbolized. War with him is destruction, inexorable cruelty, horror, death. To express that is the artist's task. The dead and dying, a terrible medley, lie on the ground in pools of blood. Blood drips from the shouldered sword of the rider whose forehead is enclosed by a brazen ring, whose features know of no pity. With an indifferent firmness which allows no escape he rides his dark horse over the fallow bodies. The gloomy, bloody red of an evening sky glows in the back — ground. — In this way Stuck gave form to what the others merely hinted at. And who will deny that this truthful work of the m o d e r n artist, this harmony of intention and execution, produces a more perfect kind of beauty than the older representations of a similar theme, where, under the influence of tradition, the artistic problem had not been exhausted?

*   *
*

After some skirmishing the literary revolution proper started in 1885. M i c h a e l G e o r g C o n r a d, a sturdy, honest, and fearless character, established a periodical D i e G e s e l l s c h a f t (S o c i e t y) which became the central organ of "youngest Germany". Although a convinced Zolaist himself — he had visited Zola in Paris and become his first prophet in Germany — Conrad opened the columns of his magazine to writers of the most varied tendencies. Anything truly "modern", i. e. vigorous, vital, sincere, was welcome to him. "What we want", so he introduced D i e G e s e l l s c h a f t, "is to restore to its place of honor the badly oppressed virility and courage in philosophy, poetry, and criticism". And he was successful. The final victory of the modern movement was largely due to Conrad's and his associates' liberal management of this one magazine. Here nearly all of those authors that a short time later came into prominence published their first-lings. Here the stupidity and malice of influential opponents met with quick and thorough executions. — As to his own productions Conrad's fame is less enduring. Neither as a poet nor as a novelist (W a s d i e I s a r r a u s c h t, 1888) he reached his own standard. He was too impassioned a fighter to ever acquire the balanced calmness of a creator.

The same thing may be said of K a r l B l e i b t r e u who from 1888 to 1890 was an editor of D i e G e s e l l - s c h a f t. After establishing his reputation by D i e s I r a e (1884), a magnificent account of the battle of Sedan, he attracted the public's attention to the modern tenden- cies with a pamphlet R e v o l u t i o n i n L i t e r a t u r e (1886). His ideas were neither new nor very clear. His judgment of older and contemporary authors was question- able. But through his impetuous attack against the conventions of the day many who had been ignorant so far now learned that a change was taking place. The interest in T h e M o d e r n s began to be general. Bleibtreu himself proved to be one of the most voluminous writers of the age, without achieving that great work which he promised in his manifesto, when he was young with the young. He, with a score of other revolutionists, contributed to M o - d e r n e D i c h t e r - C h a r a k t e r e, a collection of lyrics edited by Wilhelm Arent, Hermann Conradi, and Carl Henckell, published in the winter of 1884 to '85, and republished under the new title J u n g d e u t s c h l a n d (Y o u n g G e r m a n y) the following year. While the novel seemed entangled in foreign influences, the lyric was to be independently national. It was, so the editors proclaimed, to be "titanic" and fraught with "genius". The poets were once more to be conscious of their true mission: "to be guardians and conservators, leaders and comforters, pathfinders and guides, physicians and priests of humanity, and first of all, singers of genuine songs: songs that strike and inflame the hearts, that awaken the sleeping, that strengthen the tired, awe the sinners, scare the revellers and voluptuous from their dens, stigmatizing or reforming them. In this anthology such a group of poets have joined hands for the vow to devote themselves for ever only to this higher, nobler, and deeper conception of their art!"

Are such aims less idealistic than those of our great classics? And the "moderns" were indeed very much in earnest. There is much youthful rhetoric, much extreme hatred and negation in the volume, but there is also an abundance of social love and sympathy, of positive energy, of solid promises for the future. Conradi, the author of the above quoted words, passed away a few years later. But there were Carl Henckell, Julius Hart, Heinrich Hart, Otto Erich Hartleben, Ernst von Wildenbruch, Wolfgang Kirchbach, and Arno Holz, all men who in no small degree by their maturer work justified the expectations raised in this stormy declaration of modernism.

"Songs of a Modern" was the sub-title of a stately volume of poems B o o k o f t h e T i m e which A r n o H o l z published in 1885, soon after M o d e r n e D i c h - t e r c h a r a k t e r e. It contains the "program":

> Kein rückwärts schauender Prophet,
> Geblendet durch unfassliche Idole,
> Modern sei der Poet,
> Modern vom Scheitel bis zur Sohle!

"Let the poet be modern, modern from head to foot." In another place Holz says: "This our world is no more classic, this our world is not romantic, modern only is this

world." — Arno Holz was destined to liberate modern
German literature from foreign influences. In 1885, a mere
youth, he fully mastered the traditional forms and even
extended the range of poetry to fields hitherto neglected:
he was the leader in "metropolitan" lyrics. Better than
any of his immediate companions he carried out the above
program. But as to style he had not yet found his own.

D e t l e v v o n L i l i e n c r o n , nearly twenty years
older and a master of his craft too, with the reminiscences
of the great war-times, with the experiences of an eventful
life to draw upon, enthusiastic for progress, young in his
heart, realized in his poetry much of what the moderns were
striving for. A group of younger men gathered about him
as their beloved master: the versatile and graceful O t t o
J u l i u s B i e r b a u m , the refined G u s t a v F a l k e ,
the profound R i c h a r d D e h m e l . The latter is usually
designated as a romanticist. None of them may strictly be
classified under the heading "naturalism" or any other
"ism". They all were and are artists of high order. Their
work, together with Arno Holz's, not only justified the
modern movement but also proved once more the superiority in lyrics of the people that has produced Walter
and Goethe.

*   *
*

While the lyric, owing to its very nature as an expression of individual soul-life, rapidly outgrew the turbulent stage of strom and stress, of revolutionary purposes, the novel for a long time remained the vehicle of

discussions, chiefly social and economic, instead of developing an indigenous and harmonious style capable of representing objectively any phase of modern society. There were imitators of Zola, of Dostoyewski, of Turgeneff, of Tolstoy, but not one original German writer who could compare with the foreigners as m o d e r n artists. It is true, T h e o d o r S t o r m and G o t t f r i e d K e l l e r lived until 1888 and 1890 respectively and published their most realistic novels D e r S c h i m m e l-r e i t e r and M a r t i n S a l a n d e r after the momentous year 1885. M a r t i n S a l a n d e r even takes issue with a certain kind of modernism in Switzerland. However, both writers, with their whole personal character and novelistic technique, belong to the age that followed in the wake of Goethe and early romanticism. Likewise T h e-o d o r F o n t a n e, the famous author of anglicizing ballads, of travel-books, and novels. Writing criticisms of current literature for one of Berlin's leading papers, he was in the closest possible contact with the new movement and allowed himself to be carried along. At the age of sixty-two he composed his first m o d e r n novel: L ' A d u l t e r a (published in 1882). Fontane recognized the ideal of modern art. He was convinced that the perfection of beauty depended on truth, that there was no greater art than naturalness in speech and characterization, than pure essentiality free from mannerism and embellishments. He broke away from his own oldfashioned methods, trying to put into practice the new theory he believed in. He took for his principal theme the most delicate problem of modern society: the illegitimate liaison versus matrimony. In his best works I r r u n g e n W i r r u n g e n (1887) and E f f i B r i e s t (1895) he does away with that studied pose and moralizing subjectivism, with those decorative tableaus, which even the best of the old school had indulged in. With straightforward simplicity he tells his story, as an impartial observer and recorder of life, not as a judge nor as an orator with the applause of his audience in mind. Fontane needed only a little more vigor, more elasticity, to mean for Germany what Flaubert and Zola meant for France.

For just the opposite reason an Austrian author failed to create the new German novel: L u d w i g A n - z e n g r u b e r (1839—1889). He was possessed of such a fiery temperament that he never sufficiently succeeded in controlling it for the sake of his art. His imagination and plastic faculties were immense. In comical and serious plays, anecdotes, short stories, novels, he enriched German Literature with a variety of characters and situations worthy of the very greatest geniuses. But he lacked the cultural refinement and esthetic discrimination of Fontane, and he purposely employed his talent for the education of his people. So even in his most elaborate books, the vivid portrayals of peasant life T h e B l o t o f S h a m e (D e r S c h a n d f l e c k, 1883) and T h e S t a r s t o n e - F a r m (D e r S t e r n s t e i n h o f, 1885) pedagogy and art appear in conflict; and what Anzengruber actually accomplished is rather the completion of Gotthelf's, Ludwig's, and Auerbach's work than the beginning of something new. After all, in prosefiction this decade, with its many experiments, did not produce a single m o d e r n work that could compare with the moderately realistic novels of Ludwig, Keller, Freytag, and Scheffel. The rejuvenation of the novel came through the drama.

George II, Duke of Saxe-Meiningen, as early as the middle of the seventies gave a strong impulse toward reforming the theater. In contrast to the star-sytsem in vogue he organized the troupe of his own theater so as to insure an adequate representation of all characters, great or small. Collective playing took the place of individual virtuosity. The mass-scenes, hitherto lifeless decorations, became integral parts of the action. Costumes and setting were made historically correct. The actor who had assumed a position of superiority over the dramatist, was once more reduced to his proper rank as an interpreter of another's intentions. Shakespeare and Schiller who largely made up the repertoire of the "Meiningers", appeared in an entirely new light, putting to shame the melodramas and frivolous society-plays either imported from France or manufactured at home. Traveling through Germany and a considerable part of Europe, the Meiningen troupe trained the important theaters to appreciate sound illusionism and unity of style. In this work of theatrical education they soon were supported by the rise of Richard Wagner's music-drama, Bayreuth being opened in 1876, two years after the first performance of the Meiningers in Berlin.

Then came Ibsen, introduced by the Meiningers. In

June 1876 they played T h e P r e t e n d e r s in Berlin.
In 1878 followed P i l l a r s o f S o c i e t y , in 1880 A
D o l l ' s H o u s e , in 1887 R o s m e r s h o l m and
G h o s t s . This was the critical year for the Scandinavian's influence in Germany. The old generation rose
in arms against the dramatic anarchist, the young gathered
about him as the modern Shakespeare. The dreams of
T h e M o d e r n s seemed gloriously realized. Now the
"lies" of society received their deserved condemnation
from the highest tribunal of poetry, dramatic art; truth
at last reigned supreme. As the theory of French naturalism demanded, man and his actions appeared dependent
on environment, race, heredity. These plays were constructed on the basis of an absolutely consistent motivation.
The crutches of oratorical monologs, of scenic changes, of
direct characterization were discarded. The dialog was
life itself; never before had such genuine conversations been
heard from the stage. Art and nature seemed one, indeed.
A multitude of imitators swarmed over the country. It
was easy to grumble with the old at the Ibsen-epidemic.
It was easier still to blindly admire. To do honor to the
great man and yet remain conscious of his limitations was
a rare merit.

Fontane and Arno Holz saw through the appearance
of naturalness. They saw that there was objectivity of
nature only in so far as Ibsen had brought his personal
ideas into a perfectly logical system with dramatic motive
power. The plays as such were, in the last analysis,
no more free from subjective pathos than Schiller's. Ibsen's

world was a world viewed from the angle of little Norway, not a cosmos with unlimited vistas. Ibsen could teach German Literature much but not everything. Was it not possible to observe nature and to record her effects free from any conventions whatsoever, as if neither Ibsen's, nor Zola's, nor any other method existed? Arno Holz set about to make this experiment and, assisted by Johannes Schlaf, he discovered p l e i n - a i r for literature.

In the winter of 1887 to 1888 the two friends wrote a number of sketches, then F a m i l i e   S e l i c k e , a play of domestic life, subsequently published together under the title N e w   P a t h s   (N e u e   G l e i s e) in 1891. The critic Franz Servaes in his P r a e l u d i e n (1899) gives a classic description of the new technique: "While they were at work . . . striving for nothing else, as they thought, but to grasp life in its minutest manifestations, something strange happened. Absorbing the whole world only with their senses, so to speak, their hearing as regards human speech had heen sharpened wonderfully. Not only that they recorded dialectical differentiations far more accurately than had been the case before; they also observed and reproduced most faithfully what may be called the "mimics of speech": those little liberties and "modesties" beyond any syntax, logic, or grammar, wherein are expressed the germination and growth of a thought, the unconscious reactions to opinions and gestures of the partner, anticipation of objections, c a p t a t i o   b e n e v o l e n t i a e , and all those subtile fluctuations of the soul which the reflectors of life usually endeavored to pass over as "unimportant",

which, however, generally contain and betray the very
essence. Holz and Schlaf noting all this with the most
painstaking conscientiousness, acquired an intimacy of tone
of speech which, transferred to the drama, was bound to
revolutionize it and at the same time give it a new style."
— This technique was both indigenous and universal, embracing a wider circle, revealing more valuable treasures
of nature than was possible with the technique of the
French or Scandinavians. In its plain sincerity it did not
need to be tested by raising the vulgar and ugly to heroic
proportions, nor by abnormal problems. It was not subservient to ulterior tendencies. The social and sexual
questions, the emancipation of woman, the political constellations were no more important for it than the dreams
of a child or the motes in a sun-beam. It was not bent
upon sensational discoveries; it fulfilled its immediate duty
of depicting sections of every day life, ready for greater
tasks to come. The new technique was a revelation to the
Moderns. To it, as much as to Ibsen's method of composition, was due the rapid progress in Germany of strict
realism in drama and fiction. Gerhart Hauptmann's success
rests upon Holz's formal training.

Following the example of Antoine's t h é â t r e l i b r e
in Paris, Maximilian Harden (the afterwards famous editor
of D i e Z u k u n f t), Otto Brahm, and two others, founded
a F r e e T h e a t e r (F r e i e B ü h n e) in Berlin; that is
to say, a dramatic society that presented modern plays to
an audience of registered members. Being a private organization the F r e e T h e a t e r was exempt from censor-

2*

ship and independent of popular taste. Young talents were to be encouraged. "In the selection of dramatic works as well as in their representation the aim was to be a live art remote from conventionality and mechanical virtuosity." The repertoire of the first season, 1889/90, consisted of five foreign and three native dramas, among the former being: Ibsen's Ghosts and Tolstoy's P o w e r o f D a r k n e s s, among the latter Hauptmann's B e f o r e S u n r i s e. The controversies before and after Hauptmann's first appearance on the stage, the riot between friends and foes during the performance, the moral victory of the progressives, mark this year 1889 as another milestone in the development of M o d e r n i s m, inspite of the fact that B e f o r e S u n r i s e did not yet represent the new style in its purity. This was not done until, six months later, the F r e e T h e a t e r performed F a m i l i e S e l i c k e of Holz and Schlaf. Narrower in its scope, less glaringly radical in its subject-matter, the fundamental newness of its art-form was appreciated only by a few connoisseurs like Theodor Fontane. While the originator of the m o d e r n drama soon fell back into undeserved obscurity, his pupil reaped the harvest.

Hauptmann's fame steadily increased with each successive play, until with T h e W e a v e r s German naturalism seemed to have reached its zenith, in 1892.

The public mind linked the name and fame of another author with Gerhart Hauptmann's: H e r m a n n S u d e r - m a n n. Both were believed to stand for the same artistic

principles; both were looked upon by enthusiastic admirers
as a sort of modern Goethe and Schiller. Each had his
own special retinue of vassals who jealously guarded the
privileges of their respective masters, until Sudermann
himself stepped forward in order to crush his critics by a
series of violent polemics that appeared under the title
B r u t a l i z a t i o n   i n   d r a m a t i c   C r i t i c i s m   (V e r -
r o h u n g   i n   d e r   T h e a t e r k r i t i k) in 1902. The
result of this literary war proved quite contrary to Sudermann's intentions. Instead of saving his glory as a poet,
he opened everybody's eyes to the fact that he was no
poet at all but a skilful playwright and story-teller whose
chief purpose was to attract attention and to fill his pocket-
book. It is true, in his beginnings Sudermann came very
near being a genuine artist. After a few rather Frenchy
stories he published, in 1887, his best work: D a m e
C a r e   (F r a u   S o r g e). In this novel which contains
autobiographical elements, there is to be found, mingled
with gross superficialities, a delicacy of touch, a tenderness
of feeling, a sincerity of tone we look for in vain in his
subsequent production. With H o n o r   (D i e   E h r e),
1889, Sudermann started his downward course to mere
stage-show which was to be for ever his chief characteristic. It was an evil omen that Oscar Blumenthal (the
German equivalent of our George Ade) determined the final
version and managed the first performance of the play.
Characters and situations were modeled after the often-
tried black-and-white-method of effective contrasts. There
being added a small ingredient of new, so-called natural-

istic subject-matter, the mixture turned out to be a "hit" surpassing in extent by far Hauptmann's artistic success.

Talents were plentiful at that time. F r e e T h e a - t e r s , M o d e r n S o c i e t i e s sprang up in every nook and corner of Germany and Austria. New stars were discovered continually. The press soon found it advantageous to support the irresistible movement. Important editorial chairs were occupied by moderns. New Magazines were founded to propagate modern ideas in all phases of art and life. The publishing firm S. Fischer in Berlin started a periodical F r e i e B ü h n e (1890), and its editor-in-chief was Otto Brahm. Maximilian Harden through his Z u k u n f t (1892) made himself one of the foremost leaders in the cause of progress. There followed the satirical weeklies S i m p l i c i s s i m u s and J u g e n d (both 1895), with their staffs of brilliant writers and artists. M o d e r n i s m was no longer a problem, it was a fact, a historical epoch, a new style in literature, the fine arts, music, architecture, handicrafts.

Among the many dramatists this prolific age produced, besides Holz, Schlaf, and Hauptmann, deserve special mention: M a x H a l b e , H a n n s v o n G u m p p e n - b e r g and A r t h u r S c h n i t z l e r .

Max Halbe's enduring contribution is J u g e n d , a play that rivalled Sudermann's greatest theatrical successes without being at all theatrical. When it made its first appearance on the stage in 1893, it had the effect of a revelation. What the general public had seen of "naturalism" so far, were melancholy pictures of the war of the classes;

misery, negation, embittered criticisms of state, church, and society; reflexes of the fatalistic conception of environment, heredity, and so forth. Here was a drama that apparently had nothing to do with any system. It was a spontaneous outburst of passion, the simple story of an overpowering love, inexpressibly sweet in spite of its sad conclusion. And yet J u g e n d was peculiarly naturalistic in its form. The surroundings, landscape and national characteristics of a half-slavonic community in German Poland, a loyal German priest, his fanatically Polish assistant, a maturing boy, a warm-hearted girl, the mellow, dreamy, longing moods of spring, the inner harmony and necessity of it all: nowhere else but in naturalism could Halbe have found the colors for this beautiful picture of youth. — Never again did he reach the height of this one play, however seriously he took his art; but he remained a poet of respectable powers, a brave fighter for a good cause, one of the most sympathetic characters in recent literature.

Independent of coteries, difficult to define because of an extraordinary versatility, H a n n s v o n G u m p p e n - b e r g has not yet found the recognition due him. With M. C. Conrad, Liliencron, Bierbaum and others he organiz- ed, in 1890, a S o c i e t y f o r M o d e r n L i f e in Mu- nich. Although deeply religious, he was at one time prose- cuted for blasphemy. For publicly reciting and impartially discussing a socialistic poem by Karl Henckell, with whom he did not agree, he was imprisoned. One of the wittiest parodists and satirists of the century, he treats profound philosophical problems, in prose-essays, novels, and dramas. The poet of elegiac moods, sad disappointments, unfulfilled hopes, he writes comedies of exhilarating humor, tragedies of manly heroism. In addition to all this he is an unsurpassed translator of foreign lyrics, and a critic of that rare objectivity which is the result of knowledge, cultural refinement, and creative instinct. His most pretentious and, perhaps, most enduring works are a number of dramas from the early history of Germany. More successfully than Hauptmann in F l o r i a n G e y e r , he applied here a modified form of naturalistic technique to the drama of grand historical dimensions: K ö n i g K o n r a d I., K ö n i g H e i n r i c h I., H e r z o g P h i l i p p s B r a u t f a h r t (1904).

Grillparzer's lamentation over Vienna as "a Capua of the geniuses" may have been a pessimistic exaggeration then and may be groundless now, certain it is that, generally speaking, Austria and its capital city have produced fewer poets and artists of old-time German virility and consistency of purpose than the Fatherland. The mixture of many races seems to necessitate compromises. Tradition is stronger and, in Vienna at least, more evenly distributed among the population than anywhere beyond the black-and-yellow boundary-posts. A certain love of polished etiquette and philistine tranquility, a predilection for feminine grace, playfulness, and softness counteract revolutionary tendencies. Naturalism in Austria, then, is a compromise too. From its very beginning it did not affect principles and convictions so much as technical routine. Anzengruber's robust personality had no descendants. Arthur Schnitzler,

Vienna's most naturalistic writer, is nearer Paul Heyse than Arno Holz. He shows the unrestraint in the choice of subjects and the mastery of language associated with naturalism, but even his boldest scenes are toned down to a dangerously sentimentalizing haze so as to approach the "beautiful lie" of the old school. —

The reform of the theater infused new life into fiction. Verbosity, lyrical interpolations, clumsy structure had been the national characteristics of the German novel. Now the theater taught the force of plain directness, of the economy of expression. The author disappeared more and more from the pages of his book and with him the "gentle reader". Characters and events were made to speak for themselves. Ibsen's immanent motivation was transferred to the novel. The art of narration for the sake of entertainment developed in the direction toward a pure art of expression. The names of Georg Freiherr von Ompteda, Wilhelm von Polenz, Ludwig Thoma, and the brothers Mann, to quote only a few types, indicate so many successive stages in this course.

Ompteda in his best works, the series German Nobility about 1900: Sylvester von Geyer, Eysen, Cäcilie von Sarryn, Polenz in Der Grabenhäger try to define the relation of the "privileged classes" to the modern commonwealth. Both come to the same conclusion: the greatest and only real privilege of the true nobleman is his inherited sense of duty to king and country; the higher his rank, the higher his responsibilities. In this era of abolishing class-distinctions it is his task to maintain his place by social efficiency. As sound as the ethical standpoint of the two aristocratic authors, is their manner of representation. The impoverished gentry, the family life of wealthy nobles in the city, the patriarchical organization of a great estate, the struggle of an entire race against disintegration through worthless members- everything, the good and the bad, is reported with the trustworthy frankness of chronicles.

Two other works of Polenz's who spent the larger part of his short life in the country as a landed squire, show his intimate knowledge of the peasantry and the better middle class: Der Pfarrer von Breitendorf (1893) and Der Büttnerbauer (1895). In the former he takes issue with the problem of religion versus formalism, in the latter he describes the gradual ruin of an oldfashioned farmer by the pitiless business methods of a Jewish usurer. A keen observer, Polenz was not a poet of fascinating imagination nor of artful finesse. He is rather industrious and careful than brilliant. But so warm are his sympathies, so righteous is the trend of his thought, so reliable his recording that for a long time to come his books will be important factors in the education of his people.

As to Ompteda, many of his writings are of little value. The influence upon him of such sensualists as Marcel Prévost and Maupassant (whom he translated) was too great to keep all of his work unmarred. However, his latest novel Excelsior (1910) seems a definite turn to the seriousness of his great trilogy. It glorifies the beauties of Alpine scenery where, in communion with God's

most wonderful work, man may find health for body
and soul.

Ludwig Thoma is known the world over as an
editor of März and Simplizissimus whose spiri-
tus rector he has been for years, waging a relent-
less war against reaction in state and church, partly under
the nom de plume "Peter Schlehmil". He is less known
as an eminent artist. To be sure, his Lausbubenge-
schichten and Tante Frieda (Stories of a
Bad Boy and their sequel) are widely read and admired
for their superb humor; likewise his tale of Der hei-
lige Hies and Briefwechsel eines bayri-
schen Landtagsabgeordneten (Correspon-
dence of a Bavarian Legislator). Few there
are who appreciate the amount of poetical talent, plastic
power, artistic self-control and wisdom required to be
comical without the slightest suggestion of pose, to make
a "boy" think and speak and act like a boy with so perfect an illusion as to absolutely conceal the man-author
behind his work, the story still being of vital interest to mature readers. Such truly naturalistic objectivity Ludwig
Thoma attains in nearly all of his writings, dramatic or novelistic. Satirical or polemical they are, indeed. For too deeply
engaged in his patriotic war is Thoma to waste any of his
chances to gain new ground. His main interest lies with
the, alas!, eternal problem of ultramontanism. It is not
the catholic religion in itself, nor any other form of religion he battles against but the abuse of religion for political intrigues and worldly advantages. He would not

have Germany enslaved once more by Rome. And his country has no braver fighter in this all-important issue than he is. But he fights as an artist: creating characters in contrasting situations and making the reader draw his own conclusions. He does not preach: he reproduces life as it is. Avoiding effects, he is always sure of effect. As his Bad Boy, so his legislators, peasants, priests, lawyers, foresters, inn-keepers, servants, government-officials, policemen, soldiers, schemers, egotists, idealists, and so forth, are portrayed with a faculty of psychological identification rivalled, at present, only by Thomas Mann. The peasant-novel Andreas Vöst (1906) is perhaps Thoma's strongest book. A comparison of its terse language, clear-cut style, and solid architecture with its predecessors from Oberhof to Sternsteinhof reveals the great advance made toward that immanent beauty which, though superior to any nomenclature, would be called classic, if our generation did not so persistently clamor for new names. This new name, Modern Naturalism, rightly understood, indeed means an indigenous Classicism, a national art.

*   *

*

When Goethe made his most systematic effort to convert his Germans to Graecomania, the first Romantic School had organized. Between 1798 and 1800 both Goethe's Propyläen and the Schlegels' Athenäum appeared. In 1887 the Symbolists under Huysmans

seceded from Zola; in 1889 not only Hauptmann's B e -
f o r e S u n r i s e but also Maeterlinck's P r i n c e s s
M a l e i n e were first performed. In the same year,
owing to the sensation of his mental collapse, Friedrich
Nietzsche's romantic philosophy and poetry began to influence noticeably the new generation. The word M o -
d e r n i s m comprises both N a t u r a l i s m and S y m -
b o l i s m or N e o - R o m a n t i c i s m. As the former
was frequently misinterpreted as an art of the surface
only, so the latter in its totality was mistaken for perverse
obscurantism and playful subjectivism. The germ of
romanticism, old or new, is the assertion of intuition as over
against observation. Darwin's and Haeckel's hypothesis
of evolution claimed that during millions of years organic
life had developed from matter and that the human spirit
was the climax so far reached in that development. In
this round-about way the soul was connected with the universe by a chain perceivable to the intellect. But this kind
of rationalism had little or no emotional force for the
average individual. One needed the moral fibre of the
great scholars to console oneself with a theoretical expectation of further evolutions in a distant future. There could
not be extinguished the inveterate longing for a direct and
ever present contact with the primeval power. The individual was not contented with being an infinitesimal link
in a mechanical, if immense system. Were not God and
man one? Cosmic consciousness must be experienced in
man's own soul. And it was not only the human Ego but
also the petty occurrences of daily life, animals, and inanim-

ate objects that stood in dynamic interrelation with the Universe. Mystic contemplation once more built up a theosophical mythology. The occult arts flourished. Spiritism invaded the territory just conquered by experimental science. Naturalistic writers of all denominations yielded to the romantic reaction. They discovered the gigantic symbolism in Zola's L a B ê t e H u m a i n e, L a T e r r e etc., and Ibsen's mysterious allegorisms were likened to Maeterlinck's visions. Dream-plays, fairy-operas took turns with dramas of social revolution. Hauptmann's S u n k e n B e l l seemed to put an end to the era of naturalism.

Only external technicalities came to Germany from abroad. Baudelaire, Mallarmé, and Verlaine were translated. S t e f a n G e o r g e and H u g o v o n H o f - m a n n s t h a l whose career began about 1893, sacrificed plasticity of content to the bombastic vagueness of musical or coloristic effects p e r s e. They claim that there, is no direct road from life to poetry nor from poetry to life. Poems are to be weightless tissues of words. "A new and bold combination of words is the most wonderful gift for the soul and not inferior to a statue of the youth Antinous or to a large, vaulted gate." Not possessing vitality enough to draw poetry from real nature, they declare reality a mere phantom, a dream, a distorted reflex of the poetical soul, arriving in this way at the decadent extremes of that pseudo-romanticism which, at the beginning of the century, had developed from an exaggerated application of Fichte's subjectivism.

As to the romantic attitude of mind proper — the constant longing for a far-away ideal and the intuitive cosmic feeling — Maeterlinck was found to be an echo of N o v a l i s. He and his contemporaries regained their lost prestige. The blue flower blossomed once more on its native soil. But the phenomenal personality of F r i e d - r i c h N i e t z s c h e overshadowed all other romantic factors combined and gave neo-romanticism its stamp of modernity. T h u s S p a k e Z a r a t h u s t r a (1885) became the gospel of the romantic moderns.

No serious student of social organization to-day denies the untenableness of Nietzsche's ethics as a system on the one hand, nor the enormous positive value of its affirmative elements on the other hand. The doctrine of the determining influence of environment, the leveling tendencies of social democracy together with the perverse asceticism of Richard Wagner's last period, had spread a weakly pessimism, a sceptic despair of individual assertion which like a malicious epidemic drained the energies of the nation. Now, a trumpet-blast in the battle of life, Nietzsche's call sounds through the stifling atmosphere of negation, humiliation, discouragement. Away from the crowd of weaklings! be a master, not a slave! be thyself! forward and upward! There is the prize: instead of the liberty, equality, fraternity of indifferent average people, instead of the desolate monotony of the herd — the hero, the superman!

Nietzsche's doctrine of the superman is a curious blend of the results of Darwin's inductive evolutionism and

deductive speculation. The gradation matter, plant, animal, man: is, by virtue of romantic intuition, carried forward into the future. In the course of time mankind will
produce the superman who stands in the same relation to
the present species "man" as this to its animal ancestor.
To reach the goal of superhumanity a hard and incessant
struggle is necessary. Whoever has that ideal in his heart,
regards this present life as a station, an experiment, not as
a terminal. On the other hand he endeavours to exhaust
all possibilities of this life; he is an affirmer of life in the
highest sense; he accepts and asserts life with all its pain
and joy; he lives as if every minute were of eternal duration, for every step toward the distant ideal is a newly
conquered value in itself. The proclamation of the superman is one half of Zarathustra's mission, the other half is
the prophecy of the eternal recurrence of all things.

Zarathustra has with him an eagle and a serpent. The
eagle is the symbol of the aspiring superman, the coiled
serpent is the symbol of palingenesis. As Christianity
bases its ethics on the belief in a beyond, so Zarathustra's
ethics is based upon the belief in palingenesis here in this
our physical world. [We follow Gustav Naumann's valuable
commentary]. "How, if, of a day or night, a demon followed thee up into thy most solitary solitude speaking to thee
thus: "This life, as thou art living it and hast been living
it now, thou wilt have to live once more and innumerable
times more; and there will be nothing new in it, but every
pain and every joy, and every thought, and every sigh, and
every thing unspeakably small or great in thy life must

return to thee, and everything in the same order and
sequence — and likewise this spider and this moon-light
among the trees, and likewise this moment and myself.
The eternal hour-glass of existence will be turned again
and again — and thou with it, dust of dust!" — wouldst
thou not fall down and gnash thy teeth and curse the demon
speaking thus to thee? Or hast thou ever experienced a
grand moment, when thou wouldst reply: "thou art a god,
and never did I hear anything more divine!" If that idea
overcame thee, it would, as thou art, transform and perhaps
crush thee; the question, with each and every thing: "doest
thou wish this once more and innumerable times more?"
would lie upon thy actions as the greatest weight." —
"My doctrine says: to live so that thou must wish to live
again, is the task — for this will be so at all events! . . .
Let us not look for distant unknown beatitudes and blessings and graces, but live so that we want to live again and
live for ever in this way! . . . We want to experience a
work of art over and over again! We must shape our lives
so that we have the same desire at its individual points!
This is the thought of thoughts!"

The insoluble discrepancy between the theory of palingenesis and the theory of constant progress toward superhumanity need not be discussed here. Nor did the former
greatly influence the thought of Nietzsche's contemporaries.
What inspired them was the bracing force of his heroic
individualism and his dionysian delight in the fulness of
life. This inspiration was far more wholesome in its effect
upon the educated at large than the blind adoption of

superman-ethics was disastrous for the immature. But this will always be an open question. So much is undeniable that Z a r a t h u s t r a as poetry belongs to the greatest treasures of the world's literature. It is not an epic, as a distinguished scholar would have it, but the didactic poem of a romantic idealist. Like L e a v e s o f G r a s s, though superior to it in form and content, it is less a creation of concrete images than an oratorically beautiful expression of thoughts. But there never was more magnificent oratory, a more imposing array of striking metaphors, figures, new word-values — and deep thoughts. In judging Nietzsche we must forget the unfortunate victim of a mental disease that caused the hideous outbursts of blasphemous megalomania after Z a r a t h u s t r a. We must respect the sincerity of the healthy seeker for truth; we must admire the great poet who rejuvenated his native language as did Luther, Lessing, Goethe, and Bismarck.

II.

Detlev von Liliencron

———

If Detlev von Liliencron had been born in England, France, or Italy, the world would long have known him as one of the few great poets of our age. Being neither more nor less than a German he remained almost unnoticed. He was too noble a man to advertize himself, too genuine an artist to cater to the taste of the masses, too thorough a German to create an international sensation. He wrote three or four autobiographies. One is a novel in which he tells more of his spiritual than of his material life; in another he gives a brief account of his military career and the awakening of his genius. The third reads as follows: "Detlev Baron von Liliencron was born in Kiel on the 3rd of June 1844, took part in the wars of 1866 and 1870/71 as a Prussian officer, and lives now, a retired captain, in Alt-Rahlstedt near Hamburg."

It was "because of wounds and debts" that, upon the close of the Franco-German war, he quit the army and turned to this country hoping for a military career in Central or South America. He failed completely, altough he had certain connections with America through the family of his mother who, a daughter of General Harden, was born in Philadelphia. No less disappointed and homesick than Lenau forty years before, he soon returned to Germany, entered the civil service, and held modest positions as an administrative officer, until in 1887 he resigned to live as an independent author, still proud of his well earned title "Hauptmann". If we add that he died, a poor man, on the 22nd of July 1909, we have probably said as much as he wished the general public to know of his private affairs. "Hands off my life!", he warns his critics. The man was for ever to remain his own master; the artist alone belonged to the world.

The biographical note quoted is followed by ten poems which Liliencron himself had selected as his best.[1]) They indicate the nature and scope of his esthetic experiences: war, chase, hatred of philistinism, consciousness of life's duality, erotic passion, tender sympathies, love of nature, a romantic longing for the unattainable.

The literary reflex of Liliencron's American episode are a few fine lyrics: D e p a r t u r e , R e t u r n , and T h o u   m y   c o u n t r y ; a tragic love story the scene of which is New York, and two dramatic efforts: T h e N o b i l i t y   o f   L a b o r and P o k a h o n t a s . These as well as the plays T h e   M e r o v i n g i a n s , T r i f e l s a n d   P a l e r m o , T h e   R a n t z o w s   a n d   P o g w i s c h's , K n u t   t h e   L o r d were all written, before the poet had attained to that perfect mastery of form which characterizes his lyrics. They are painfully amateurish. With the exception of the first one mentioned each contains enough dramatic elements to make half a dozen effective plays: unbounded ambition, base envy, demonic jealousy, cold-

---

[1]) Cf. Deutsche Lyrik der Neuzeit, Leipzig 1906/07, pp. 71 ff.

blooded assassinations crowd the scenes. But what there
is of dramatic possibilities is suffocated by an overgrowth
of lyricisms and epic narrations. The plays are successions
of past events, sometimes fascinatingly told in dialogic form,
rather than present unfoldings of inner conflicts, of causes
and effects. "Tell me now", begins T h e M e r o v i n -
g i a n s. This is typical.

While his dramas share all the conventional faults
of a rhetorical age, Liliencron's war poetry is distinguished
by the strict conciseness, concrete plasticity, and directness
of imagery that mark the modern epoch of German Literature. It is the lyrics and short stories of an A d j u -
t a n t ' s R i d e s that made Liliencron one of the admired
leaders of Y o u n g e s t G e r m a n y.

The year of 1870/71 with its glorious victories and
magnificent political achievements had not found an adequate reflex in the literature immediately following it.
One or two poems by Julius Wolff and old Freiligrath
were not particularly poor but in the same declamatory
vein as the academic sonnets and songs of such men as
Geibel, Dahn, and Redwitz whose patriotism was greater
than their creative power. Liliencron, however, had not
only been, every inch of him, a soldier, had not only received highest honors for bravery and welcomed the re-estab-
lishment of the Empire with the enthusiasm of a loyal
vassal: but he had, in the very field, let the heroic emotions
of war impress him with their terribly grandiose beauty,
and had instinctively sought to give them form. "Even in

heaven I should like to take part in a battle now and then"
— a casual remark of his, worthy of an ancient Teuton.

His whole life is permeated with the ardent yearning
for the active life of a soldier. Into peaceful idyls burst
the dazzling flashes of weapons, sound drums and fifes,
thuds the rhythm of marching battalions. War is the
great, the all-important event for both the man and the
poet: the defense of king and country, the ever ready
sacrifice of one's own blood for others, the fearless equation
of life and death, the utmost exertion of all energies, the
resolute deed; and the shadows: villainous treachery,
barbarous cruelty, fiendish destruction of homesteads and
maturing crops.

A b a c k w a r d g l a n c e (R ü c k b l i c k) expresses
the sentiments before, during, and after a battle. When
the attack is about to be made, the poet's thoughts wander
back to the fairyland of childhood, to the wild life of the
man of the world. Then comes the quick plunge into
bloody combat — peril, wounds, victory. After all is over,
in the night, by the gleaming campfire, the musings of the
morning are continued, to be dissolved into the elating
consciousness that the fierce encounter has led the restless
youth to firm manhood. The battle itself fills only six
brief strophes. There is nothing said directly of the
thousands taking part. The figure of the individual alone
appears in sharp outlines; and yet our imagination easily
rounds the segment out to a circle. Landscape, men, objects are designated by their most characteristic names and

set in motion by means of a few verbs, scarcely any explanatory adjectives being required.

D e a t h i n t h e g r a i n f i e l d (T o d i n Ä h r e n), R e m i n i s c e n c e (I n E r i n n e r u n g), T h e C e l e - b r a t i o n (S i e g e s f e s t), each consisting of three short stanzas, show this technique still more perfected. A soldier, mortally wounded, unnoticed by the ambulances, dies after two nights and days of dreadful agony, among the ripening wheat. A fleeting vision of joyful harvest days at home, and his soul is relieved. The other two poems are constructed upon similar contrasts : here brilliant lights, the ecstasy of victory, of triumphant life ; there extreme misery, horror, death, darkness.

Such limitation of horizon, such condensation of material is the secret of Liliencron's art. It is the suggestive force of personal life that creates the impression of world-wide reality.

In his war stories he never attempts to describe a battle in its entirety, as did e. g. Grabbe, Bleibtreu, and Frenssen. What he does is this : he narrates most graphically a connected series of important actions, shows their effect upon their immediate vicinity, and concludes with a grand finale. Consequently we, his readers, go through all the thrilling experiences in one part of the battlefield, constantly realizing that, at the same time, similar scenes take place everywhere around us, until at last the isolated details merge into their combined result, into the all-embracing catastrophe. So, as our attention was never distracted, as our eyes were not compelled to stray over an

endless procession of images, a few images are clearly
and permanently inscribed upon our souls with the ultimate
effect of one overwhelmingly great phenomenon.

Horrible as many or most of these war-stories are —
Liliencron can, indeed, be appreciated only by men and
women of strong minds — the mild light of humor is not
altogether missing, nor is the spirit of love. Quite in contrast to Zola, Daudet, and Maupassant with their f a n a -
t i c exaggerations and falsifications, Liliencron never
utters a word of hatred against the enemies of his people.
True to his aristocratic name, he is always chivalric and
admires the tenacious energy, the daring é l a n of the
opposing army as much as the bravery of his own. "The
enemy's wonderful army", he once exclaims in purely
esthetic delight. Nowhere in French war literature do
we find episodes as conciliating as this: In T h e T r a c k -
m a n ' s S t a t i o n (D a s W ä r t e r h ä u s c h e n) a dying
French officer confides the secret of his life to a wounded
German. No explanations are necessary between the
two who a few moments before stood opposite each other
in a murderous fight; a steady glance from eye to eye
— they are comrades now. That is all.

In his poems and stories of war — always, in fact
— Liliencron places man in close contact with nature.
The dismal moods of rainy weather, the manifold hues
of sunsets, the splendor of starry nights, the chaste brisk-
ness of the hour before sunrise, the heat of summer
afternoons, the majestic flight of a heron through clouds
of mist far above advancing cavalry, the playful flutter

of butterflies among the bleeding wounds of the fallen —
such motives contribute essentially toward visualizing the
action proper, either by contrasts of color and light or
by plastic symbolization.

Liliencron has often been praised for his extraordinary keeness of observation. Indeed, the soldier, the hor-
seman, the hunter had his senses trained to extreme acute-
ness. Like an Indian on the warpath he seems to hear
and see everything. But it is not only, as overwise and
underread critics would have it, the detached detail, the
surface of things which he grasps. The external, individual
phenomenon has always a deeply typical meaning for him.
A prose sentence reads: "I trot through the delicious moonlit night. I trot and trot. A long trot for miles, through
the moonlit summernight. World, oh World, how fair
thou art! I trot in English fashion, I swing myself, I ride
as though in Heaven . . . Nirwana . . ." This experience,
cast into the mould of beautifully imitative rhythms,
becomes one of Liliencron's very best poems: A t w o
m i l e t r o t (Z w e i M e i l e n T r a b). The first and the
last two strophes may illustrate the suggestive force of
realistically plain imagery fraught with profound significance:

> Es sät der Huf, der Sattel knarrt,
> Der Bügel jankt, es wippt mein Bart,
> In immer gleichem Trabe.
> — — — — — — —
>
> Und wohlig weg im gleichen Maß
> Daß ich die ganze Welt vergaß,
> Im Trabe, Trabe, Trabe.

Und immer fort, der Fackel zu,
Dem Torfahrlicht der ewgen Ruh,
Im Trabe, Trabe, Trabe.

When as an adjutant he has to carry an important
message from one part of the battlefield to another, he is
stopped by a wounded soldier. His heart goes out to the
poor wretch whom a drop of water might save. But there
stands Dame Duty, solemnly commanding: "Forward!" to
save the thousands instead of the one. A vision, a dream,
and yet the very essence of present reality. "Forward,
look not behind you!", this cruelly saving call that sounded
to him so often amidst the ghastly slaughter of battle,
became the motto of his whole life. It guarded him against
W e l t s c h m e r z , that despair over the world's irreparable misery to which sensitive natures so easily
succumb.

Liliencron was a passionate hunter, not because
he enjoyed killing, but because chase kept awake in him
the chivalric virtues of war, gave constant exercise to body
and mind, and brought about the most intimate communion
with nature. On horseback or on foot, accompanied by his
faithful dogs, rambling through the solitude of heath,
marshes, and woods means ever new revelations of beauty
to him. And as war, so chase assumes symbolical significance. Wolfhunting and heron-hawking, brilliantly
depicted in two pendants, F e u d a l , change through
almost imperceptible irony into symbols of social evolution.
The modern poet revives the memory of ancestral times,
when a serf's life meant no more than the life of a wild
beast.

Another time coursing becomes a gruesome Dance of Death. Led by a grey-hound, cavalier and lady pursue in wild haste a miserable hare. The fast hound is Death himself to whom fall a prey woman and game alike.

Similarly a prose-sketch H e t z j a g d is an allegory of human life. A motley cavalcade of hunters marches past our eyes: first Fortuna. "She looked behind her, laughing, laughing, laughing so that the little gold crown upon her head glistened and sparkled." She is followed by an endless procession of woes and passions. "All that is inflicted upon man by himself and others, disease and distress, misery and want, all and everything, move by, the horses always in rapid gait." The most horrible of all vexations is Poverty, and in the same line with her comes Care; then follow Hatred, Revenge, Calumny, Scorn, Grudge, Jealousy, and, singled out as one of the very meanest, "she with the face of an old spinster, in a lilac-colored dress with a grassy green bow in her hair": Thoughtless Gossip. Close upon her comes Gambrinus, the curse of the nation, the god of the Schützen-and-Sängerfest-Germans, the god of those Philistines who despise whatever is original, whose stupid apathy causes the ruin of poets and artists. Last is Satan with his two mistresses Falsehood and Infamy. The scene is shifted for a moment. The procession seems to be transformed into an advancing regiment of cavalry. Military signals and orders are heard which are suddenly relieved by hunting-cries. Again appear the Vices and Cares. They are chasing a man. In the forest stands Adam, the man who is you and I, naked,

lonely. Frantic terror seizes him, when he hears the wild
chase approach. He knows that he is the game. He runs,
hard pressed by the bloodthirsty pack. An abyss bars his
way. He glides down the slope, clings despairingly to the
edge. But Fortuna, still leading, leaps from her horse,
and tramples upon his fingers. He sinks, falls, is lost.
Now Fortuna, waving her hand, gives the signal for a
general shout of triumph. — Slowly, from the distance,
Satan upon his elephant draws near. He takes his time;
for he is sure of success.

This somewhat lengthy extract is given, since the
content comprises an essential part of Liliencron's philosophy, and since the method of composition applied here
is used over and over again. With a rigidly realistic technique he expresses romantic sentiments. No poetry in
recent times contains a greater number nor a greater
variety of visions than his who is labeled as a naturalistic
writer. This bold vision of the wild chase grows out of a
most accurately observed, trivial reality. The time is a
weary, hot September afternoon. The scene changes
between woods and bush, where the author is engaged in
grouse-hunting, and a village-tavern. The model of Fortuna is a buxom waitress who does not dislike flirting. Yet
the moods of sunny day and spectral apparitions do not,
except once, neutralize each other. Both intermingle,
supplement each other as insensibly as in Grillparzer's
dream play.

The vision comes very near the sublime without being
wholly sublime. Liliencron rarely mastered the gesture

of solemnity. Here, in what is only a sketch — Ü b u n g s -
b l a t t — he did not want to. Humor and irony relieve
the tragic tension. Jolly flirtation introduces, unconscious
drollery of the girl closes the vision. There is one real
break, however. An unveiled personal confession separates
this sketch from pure art to which its subject points. The
horror of the Gambrinus-worshipping German philistine
misleads our poet here as elsewhere to direct polemics.
An enthusiastic patriot, he hated, as relentlessly as did
Friedrich Schlegel or Brentano, the worst enemy of his
people, the philistine who, over beer and skat, forgets the
ideals of liberty and energetic activity; who strangles with
his envy whatever is great, original, natural, in order that
he may not be disturbed in his dull indolence; the philistine
who is the absolute negation of creative spirit.

Another work T h e w a n d e r e r i n t h e h e a t h
(H a i d e g ä n g e r) is in part devoted to the struggle
against philistinism which appears in the manifold disguises
of the beerdrinking burgher, the petrified alexandrine aca-
demician, the hypocritical moralist, the faultfinding, pedan-
tic critic. D e r H a i d e g ä n g e r, in the form of Goethe's
doggerel verse, contains one of Liliencron's frankest con-
fessions. It, too, is a combination of daylight-reality and
dusky visions. The succession of apparitions is rather arbitrary; they do not constitute a coherent group as does the
wild chase.

After the philistines are disposed of, the poet finds
consolation in the arms of "Haidehanne". She, the sturdy,
brisk child of the common people is to him the personifi-

cation of healthy nature herself, to whom he flees from the distress of life. Her unselfish love gives him ever new strength and courage. Left alone again, the wonders of the heath exert their enchanting powers upon him, until he is attacked by the nightmare of maddening doubt. Then Death comes to take him along. But he is not ready to surrender. To lure him away from the world Death reminds him of its baseness, pettiness, envy, selfish hard-heartedness, of woman's fickleness and vileness, of the bitter pains of love, of his own sins, of his people's ingratitude. But the poet does not waver. Life's call is yet too strong. Haidehanne returns and drives Death away.

A last apparition attemps to sow disunion in his own heart. It is his double who accuses him of having wasted his life by immoderate indulgence. The poet is firm. If he repents anything, it is that he did not make use of all opportunities to taste from the cup of life. Like Nietzsche he has courage enough to live a second time through all joys and sorrows of the world. But, die if he must, let it be the quick death of a soldier. And this wish is granted. Again the poet finds himself among his old regiment opposite the enemy. The beloved cavalry signals sound — so full of poetry to him! —. A desperate struggle rages. Here, too, is the motto: "forward! look not behind you!" The death wound in his breast, he falls, calling for his Hanne. Leaning against her bosom, supported by nature's ever enduring vitality, his individual existence is extinguished. His last thought is devoted to his magnificent, dearly beloved fatherland.

In the two last mentioned works the bitterness of the artist's lonely fight against philistinism, and the ardor of his desire for a life of action occasionally cause a too personal form of expression. The four short strophes of O u t c r y (S c h r e i) represent the purely esthetic essence of the underlying sentiments. All that the chivalrous aristocrat, the warrior, the hunter, the man of active energy, has to oppose to the barren indifference of the senseless masses, we find here condensed into one soulstirring appeal to life and liberty.

II.

War, chase, and love are the "three green spots" Liliencron has discovered in the arid sands of life. In his erotic poetry there is no trace of that withered morbidity which has been ascribed to his epoch with more or less justification; nothing hysterically incensed — and no carnal pruriency covered up by pretentious spiritualism. Liliencron is equally far remote from D'Annunzio as from D. G. Rossetti. He is natural; strongly sensual, and at the same time capable of most delicately graded feelings. As for all great creators, the sexual passion is for him the center and source of his emotional life. In it he finds the hope for the permanency of the race, while he is painfully conscious of the transience of individual existence, of individual happiness in love. In accordance with his own sensuality he believes that man's nature is polygamic, woman's on the contrary monogamic: their mutual interests consequently never fully agree; happiness is limited to brief periods. His love-poetry has, then, of necessity a tragic undertone which, however, so rarely makes itself heard directly that professional criticism for a long time failed to notice it at all. Liliencron seemed the happy-go-lucky Epicurean, Don Juan, "Naturbursche". And it is only since his death that current opinion has begun to change to a deeper understanding, especially through the efforts of Liliencron's friends Richard Dehmel and Otto Julius Bierbaum. To both of these the present writer is indebted in many ways.

Among the selections of Deutsche Lyrik der Neuzeit one is entitled Stammelverse nach durchwachter Nacht (Stammering verses after a sleepless night). The long night with its lonely waiting draws to an end and is relieved by the sobering coolness of a dewy morning. Up from the river creak the oars of a rowboat. A thrush sings to the hearkening silence. Through the silver-grey dawn gleams the bright red of a geranium patch. The volcanic fire of erotic passion, the storm of lust and caprice is subdued. The demons of the night are dispelled by the rising sun: "humbly, as though with cast-down eyes everything awaits the day."

Forced resignation is contrasted by the fulfillment of bliss. The expression of morning-moods after the enjoyment of love is Liliencron's special forte. In variations of this theme he is as inexhaustible as the medieval minnesingers. But his instinct for the different shades of

atmosphere, light, color, sound is infinitely finer. His
T a g e l i e d e r are the most exquisite of their kind. The
sweet secrecy of night, the stealthy return of the lover in
the early morning, the quickened heart-beat in the ecstasy
of personal happiness which extends into blissful sympathy
with awakening nature, or the reluctant preparations for
another day among indifferent people — for all that he finds
such graceful words and rhythms as to disarm even the
strictest puritan.

Charming idyls, often enlivened by delightful humor,
take turns with melancholy motives. Love, with Liliencron, as a rule flames up suddenly, kindled by the magic
touch of the elves' queen. Man and woman are drawn into
each other's arms by an irresistible magnetism. The
moment is grasped, bliss enjoyed; for it escapes those that
tarry. It vanishes soon enough, at best. Happiness is
always short. Either the lovers are separated by the same
uncontrollable fate which united them, or the man is unable
to bind himself permanently, or envy and jealousy of others
are the cause of disunion. Repeatedly the poet sounds the
warning to guard the secret. For thief Envy will not rest,
until he has robbed you of your treasure. But if you hesitate
at the call of happiness, if you do not make use of an
opportunity, you will be punished by everlasting grief over
the irretrievable. The sorrow for bliss once enjoyed and
then lost is mild compared to the bitter repentance for
opportunities unused. Nothing is more terrible than a
"too late".

Even in a higher world, on the star Aldebaran, where

4*

men are better than upon this planet, where there is more
love, more forbearance, more patience, where misunder-
standings are impossible — even there happiness, once
forfeited, cannot be regained. This is the theme of one
of the poet's most richly colored, most imaginative and
sublime visions. Its principal motive recurs in the modest
garb of a song in popular vein. The sound of Poe's "never
more" is familiar to Liliencron too. But it is not the
awful raven which crooks to a feverstricken decadent; it is
the sweet little yellow-bunting with its two clear notes.
"Often", we read in one of the short-stories, "I thought:
does Beethoven perhaps unconsciously owe the beginning
of his fifth symphony to this little bird? "The knoking at
the door of fate' "?

> Kleiner Vogel, Gelb und Braun
> Mustert dein Gefieder.
> Immer klingt aus jedem Zaun
> Nur dein Liedchen wieder:
> Nimmer, nimmer, nimmer, nimmer mehr.
>
> Kleiner Vogel, Glück und Traum
> Floh wie deine Flügel.
> Bringt ein wenig Glück und Traum
> Noch im Flug dein Flügel?
> Nimmer, nimmer, nimmer, nimmer mehr.

With such simple means, with miniature paintings,
Liliencron sometimes creates far deeper effects than with
his world-embracing phantasies, however brilliant their
display of colors may be. Is it possible to express the
longing for happiness lost more simply, more intensely,
more ultimately than with the following which seems a

mere nothing, which is in reality everything, because it is all a concrete image?

Maienkätzchen, erster Gruß,
Ich breche dich und stecke dich
An meinen alten Hut.

Maienkätzchen, erster Gruß,
Einst brach ich dich und steckte dich
Der Liebsten an den Hut.

Liliencron would not be a noble man, if he had satisfied his craving for happiness by excess or by violating the rights of others. Upon his banner he has inscribed the great word "Selfcontrol". Sensuous he was, but not a libertine. He did not go astray with Robert Burns whose lyrics are rivalled in naturalness by his. With all his polygamic instinct he recognized monogamy as the pillar of social organization. His own married life he praised as the source of his highest bliss. The poet of those impassioned S t a m m e l v e r s e at the same time sung the naive charms of child-life. A soothing, fine lullaby, sweet, free from weakly sentimentality, closes the circle of his love-poetry.

Out of his family sense grows social sympathy. No one took the misery of the common people more to heart than this son of a feudal race. The tragic ballad of a tramp whom starvation drives to suicide, is a severe condemnation of the wrongs of our economic system. However, here too, in this ever present war for mere existence, the harsh command must be heeded: "Forward, look not behind you!" The desirability of universal love he ac-

knowledged, its possibility he denied as a Utopia. His
heart was governed by the same logic as Nietzsche's which
demands moderation even in charity. Like Nietzsche he
despises "society", admires the leading geniuses. Hanni-
bal, Julius Caesar, Frederic the Great, are his favorites.

The dilemma between our sympathetic instincts and
the necessity of eternal struggle is insoluble. Liliencron
is too honest to deceive himself and others with a compromise. In his opinion God's angels are asleep for this
world. Today, too, men would betray and crucify Jesus
who was love personified. Nay, in His very name they
carry on the horrid war of all against all. The angel of
peace wades in a sea of blood. — Not believing in a transcendental conciliation and adjustment of these discrepancies, Liliencron knows of only one safeguard against paralyzing scepticism: his country.

It would take a book to give an approximately
adequate idea of the variety of Liliencron's lyrics. His
balladry can only be mentioned. He occupies a place of
honor with Germany's greatest writers of ballads. Historical subjects, tragic or humorous, he treats with as great
perfection as the uncanny supernatural, which merges
into hazy dusk, or the glaring light of everyday reality.
Murder and revenge, punishment for long forgotten
crimes, violent abductions, barbarous feuds, battles, sur-
prises from ambush, destruction of cities, death-defying
defense of personal freedom, love-adventures, heroic self-
sacrifice — in brief we find all the traditional motives of
balladry. But to all he has given the impress of his own

graphic style. Even in his old age he succeeded in immortalizing events from Germany's African war.

Whatever he possessed of dramatic talent came to life in his ballads. In a few lines he gives the presuppositions together with the first steps of the action which then moves in breathless haste to its climax. There are no epic intermissions, nor rhetorcial devices for superficial decorations. Here as everywhere the expression is rigidly concise; the final effect that of some elemental force. A poem like Bürger's L e o n o r e would have been reduced by Liliencron to one half of its length. These merits were recognized very early. Liliencron often and justly complained of the apathy of his people. The author of the A d j u t a n t e n r i t t e and B a l l a d e n has long been received into the company of its classics.

III.

About one half of Liliencron's stories treat of erotic subjects. They are partly clothed in historical garb, reading like ballads in prose, partly they are taken from the life of modern society. As with the poems there is a tragic undertone common to all: a last greeting from the deathbed of a deserted girl and late repentance of the seducer; adultery, abduction and cruel retaliation, bitter resignation, mortal jealousy between father and son, brutal revenge of a disappointed rival, the touchingly modest love-token of a poor maid, and so forth. The transition to the group of a more general character is made by

the tragi-comical story of Major Glöckchen who
forfeits the love of a beautiful woman, letting himself be
duped by a wily priest. Then there are incidents from the
eventful past of the North, foremost a monumental account
of the heroic deed of the Diethmarsch peasantry at Hem-
mingstedt, where a few hundred of them annihilated a
strong army of Danish and Holstein nobles.

Hardly ever the poet attains or strives for the uniformity of structure usually expected of the Novelle.
Hunting or leisurely rambling through fields and woods,
in some indifferent country-inn, conversing with friends,
he seems to pick up his stories. Often the frame attracts
as much attention as the picture itself. As in Hetzjagd,
dream and reality, present and past, intermingle. The
poet's imagination builds bridges from the Holstein forests
to the streets of New York, from his tavern to the age of
Charles V. If the whole is sometimes rather dismembered,
if there are uninteresting interludes, there are always
charmingly vivid details. Liliencron is at his best, when-
ever he sins against the rule of objective narration, when-
ever he appears in persona, telling us of his own emotions. He is not like his fellow-countryman, Theodor Storm,
a lyric poet and a novelist at once. He is always a lyricist
who, owing to his marvellous power of visualizing, occasionally, as if by chance, may produce great epical effects.
His war-stories, then, came to be his best epic performances, not so much because of a truly narrative talent, as
because his personal feelings were identical with the outer
events.

Only one of the other stories is of equal value: T h e
M a r l p i t (D i e M e r g e l g r u b e), and this is, resembling Strindberg's wonderful L o n e s o m e , a lyric poem
in prose. An artistically sensitive man has been tied down
for thirty long years to the mechanical life of a government
official in a small town. Surrounded by a bourgeois society
he has more and more become inwardly isolated. An
unassuming bit of nature, a deserted marlpit, is his only
friend. There alone he feels free. There he can commune
with his own thoughts. And these are the old riddles:
What is this life for? Will there ever be unrestricted liberty,
perfect happiness? What is eternity? He finds no answer.
He seeks faith, and can only pray: "Lord, help my unbelief."
At last the mysterious waters of the marlpit give him peace.

An everyday subject, a commonplace landscape, but
adorned by the most delicate charms of varying moods, by
an enchanting scale of coloristic effects. The heavy melancholy is not depressing, since what we see is not the unre-
sisting defeat of a weakling. Affirmation of life has long
enough fought in him against resignation. His suicide is
not a cowardly shirking of duties, but rather the natural
end of a man who, in the course of severe struggles has
reached the limits of his earthly perception and goes, because this world certainly has nothing more to offer him —
the unknown beyond perhaps everything.

The misunderstood artist, the lonely dreamer, the
godseeker is Liliencron himself. Especially during the
years of his official career melancholy sorely afflicted him
without ever gaining the upper hand. For he possessed

one quality which he did not attribute to his hero: humor and irony which are superior to life's meanness.

Another phase of Liliencron's experiences is represented by the novel B r e i d e H u m m e l s b ü t t e l. This is the story of a sanguine man who in the wantonness of youth squanders a fortune, loses his position in the army, and, assisted by his brave, highminded wife, works his way up again from deepest humiliation and poverty. He learns self-control, retrieves his guilt, and is worthy of new happiness, when he dies rescuing a child from an approaching train. Atonement for past sins by unselfish deeds was the central idea of the poem R ü c k b l i c k which may be considered the nucleus of this novel.

T h e M a e c e n a s (Der Mäcen) and L i f e a n d L i e (Leben und Lüge) are, though written at different periods, two closely connected parts of an autobiographical romance. Born an aristocrat, destined for a life of luxury, unlimited enjoyment, and absolute freedom, Liliencron was condemned by fate to pressing poverty. Until the very last his creditors pursued him. The burden of his debts was one of the spectres that tormented him, that threatened to set him at variance with himself. Only in the dreams of his yearnings he found harmony. The maecenas is an immensely rich count — von Gadendorp — who governs his large domains as a sovereign lord. He has traveled over the whole world; has enjoyed every kind of pleasure; has never denied himself the fulfillment of any desire. He could be a tyrant, if he pleased, exploiting his subjects. But he is, like the hero of T h e M a r l p i t, a lover of the good and beautiful. Nature, his horses and dogs, the animals of the forests, are parts of his own self. He is a fatherly friend of his peasants and citizens. To mitigate want and misery is his greatest joy: "ach, schenken, schenken, könnt' ich immer schenken! Und lindern, wo die Not, die Armut haust!" so we read in another place. In artists he takes the greatest interest. He helps actors, painters, poets to succes; not by giving petty alms from time to time, but by sums of lasting value. In his will he bequeathes the bulk of his fortune to a foundation for the benefit of German authors. His diary contains his ideas on art and literature. Everything that is original, true, genuine, he approves disregarding all conventions. Whatever is sweetish and written with an eye on the public he condemns: "Who is a poet? Well, first of all a man who, impelled by his heart, writes for himself alone and only for his own pleasure . . . How? Do we poetize in order to please others? If so, we are not poets but acrobats."

While in T h e M a e c e n a s no attempt was made toward connected narration, L i f e a n d L i e is intended to be a "biographical novel". Nevertheless it is very deficient as regards its structure. It was not given to Liliencron to carry out long compositions. The title is due to his love of antitheses and alliterations. A parallel to Goethe's D i c h t u n g u n d W a h r h e i t (F i c t i o n a n d T r u t h) suggests itself; but Liliencron did not, of course, think of competing with "The Only", as he calls Goethe. "Life" is (with some modifications) the development of a dreamy, lonely boy to a brave soldier, an ardent lover, a moderately happy husband and father who, in the evening of his life becomes a lonely visionary again. "Lie" is the material splendor of his environment: the wealth of the generous maecenas who ultimately, like Faust, finds his greatest satisfaction in reclaiming sterile land and making poor people economically independent. At the close of the novel the hero, Kai, expresses his conviction that all existence is mere lie, deceptive appearance; that men never show their true characters, but masks, for otherwise they would devour one another as the animals do.

Like most of Liliencron's prose this novel, too, is interspersed with things which, having little or nothing to do with the plot, serve only to illustrate the hero's literary taste or the trend of his thought: War reminiscences, aphorisms, poems by himself or others, historical data, letters, even a complete novelette. Still, the whole book is filled with one sweet, melancholy mood. It is the retrospect of a wise man over a long life with moments of heavenly bliss and decades of unfulfilled yearning. In T h e M a r l p i t the hero once goes to meet the sun with outstretched arms. Here the distant star Aldebaran appears again and again mysteriously luring — it is in quest of this star that Kai meets death which is — perhaps the gateway to a new life or to a return home.

In a chapter "Something about poetry" Liliencron characterizes himself as an artist. The majority of his writings, he thinks, will perish with his person; only one will survive: P o g g f r e d. "In this will be perceived the irony of life; and a later period will find in it many expe-

riences of our time: the philistine pettiness of every day
life; the social, moral, and religious hypocrisy; the cowardly
negation of all strong instincts; the none the less un-
checked flight of individual imagination; the indelible
pleasure in mere existing, in the adventures of love, of war,
and travel; first of all, however, the unrestrained humor
of a perfectly independent man of the world who defies
every meanness of human fate with the formula: 'Je m'en
fiche!' Therefore, he believes, P o g g f r e d will sometime
be recognized as a landmark of brave irony."

Liliencron was no doubt too modest. The indications
are that not only P o g g f r e d will continue to live but also
a stately number of his ballads and love-poems. As a composition P o g g f r e d, which the author calls an epos, is
no less imperfect than the novels. The work, nominally
consisting of twenty-nine cantos, is in fact a collection of
separate ballads, visions, realistic idyls, grotesques, meditations. The connection established consists only in the
identity of the author and in the metrical system: groups of
ottave-rime alternate with groups of terza-rime. Indeed,
there is the refreshingly courageous irony; for the poet
was an affinity of Byron's whose Don Juan he cherished.
This is a personal union, as it were, not an esthetic unity.
However, many individual parts are of inimitable beauty.

The intelligent reader will not cease to admire the
profusion of visions, the brilliancy of colors, the melodious-
ness of rhythm, the plasticity of characters, the smoothness
and vitality of language. These verses reach up and down
the entire scale from sublime tragedy to the exuberant

frolic of carnival. And the poet builds up his imaginary castle Poggfred, where, secure from the world, he reigns over the world by force of his phantasy, so concretely that fiction is changed to truth. This wealthy grand seigneur and tiller of his own soil, this hotblooded Epicurean and humble devotee of nature, this earnest godseeker and frivolous cynic, this lonely misanthrope and brave fighter in life's struggles, this romantic dreamer and realistic artist, this melancholy humorist, this freeest of all free men: the poet and hero of P o g g f r e d is Detlev von Liliencron.

III.

Richard Dehmel

———

I.

Richard Dehmel is a more tenacious thinker than his friend Liliencron and probably for this reason seemed to him the greater artist. Both recognized and felt life's duality equally strongly. Liliencron despaired of a solution and represented the discrepancy as an eternal riddle. As a thinker he did not develop a synthetic system, a fact that has met with considerable criticism on the part of writers who are unable to see the difference between poetry and philosophy. As a lyric artist he found a perfect expression for his experiences. Liliencron is a pure creator and, within his own sphere, unsurpassed. — Dehmel, a more optimistic nature, deliberately set out in quest of the Holy Grail. His writings reflect the long and complex process of his spiritual struggles; they are, consequently, heavy, mystical, problematical, and comparatively seldom attain to the classical finish of Liliencron's poems. No author ever was more stubbornly resisted, more cynically ridiculed by one part of the press, more extravagantly praised, more sincerely idolized by the other, than Dehmel. His first books were condemned as diabolically immoral, blessed as the revelation of a new religion. To-day we are in the position to judge impartially. No one who really knows his work can doubt the profound seriousness of Dehmels aspirations. We may deny him the name of a true prophet. We must acknowledge him to be an imposing personality and an artist of high achievements.

His autobiography in D e u t s c h e   L y r i k   d e r   N e u z e i t reads as follows: "I was born on the 18th of November 1863, in Wendish-Hermsdorf near the Spree-wald, as the eldest son of a forester. First I attended the public school at Kremmen, then the Sophiengymnasium at Berlin, then the city gymnasium at Danzig. Studied Philosophy, Natural Sciences, and Social Economics, from 1882—'87, mostly in Berlin . . . Took the doctor's degree at Leipzig with a thesis on insurance; was then, until 1895, secretary of the union of German Fire Insurance Companies. While holding this office I published my first three books of poems (R e d e m p t i o n s — L o v e ' s   C h a o s — L e a v e s   o f   L i f e) and assisted in founding the artists' society P a n. Lived then in Pankow near Berlin; wrote there, having given up my position, the books of poems W o m a n   a n d   W o r l d and a new edition of R e d e m p t i o n s, the tragi-comedy T h e   F e l l o w - m a n, the pantomimic drama L u c i f e r, and, together with my first wife, the children's book F i t z e b u t z e. In 1899 I traveled about with my second wife, lived mostly abroad until 1902 (Italy, Greece, Switzerland, Holland, England), and then settled down in Blankenese near Hamburg. There I finished the epic M a n   a n d   W o m a n; perfected T h e   T r a n s f o r m a t i o n s   o f   V e n u s, wrote the children's poems T h e   L i t t l e   H e r o and a

play F i t z e b u t z e , organized with Arno Holz the cartel
of lyric authors, and prepared a collective edition of my
writings. This is about to appear (C o l l e c t e d W o r k s
in ten volumes, published by S. Fischer in B e r l i n) and
will be completed in three years."

The edition appeared, indeed, very promptly, although
the poet thoroughly revised its whole content. In the
preface he says: "A few of the books, especially L o v e ' s
C h a o s and L e a v e s o f L i f e , have been changed
almost into the reverse of their original conception." This
points to two things: first, we have to do with a power
which, in the Emersonian sense, draws the consequences
from its own development and, free from self-conceit, dis-
cards definitely views recognized as untenable. Second,
systematizing reasoning, abstract intellectuality, is in this
author at least as strong as the faculty of intuitive feeling.
The question then arises, whether or not he will, in his
poetry, be able to express in concrete form what he has
logically thought out, endowing his ideas with the sympathetic heat of vital experience. And, will he who is so
regardless of his own productions, respect the rights of
others?

It is worth noting that Maeterlinck, in the preface to
a new edition of P r i n c e s s M a l e i n e , calls attention
to the faults of his early work, at the same time declaring
changes impossible, because any revision would destroy
the charms peculiar to youth. In Dehmel the reader will
seek in vain for the delicate fragrance of youth. He never
possessed, at least he never shows, the sweet freshness of

naïveté. As a precautious, gloomily philosophizing fighter he makes his debut. An extraordinarily sensuous nature, he finds himself entangled in the orgies of a brutal eroticism, incensed by all passions and lusts. To him seem allotted neither the naively physical enjoyment of primitive man nor the spiritual peace of the civilized idealist. So strong are his animal instincts that he cannot negate them without denying himself. So strong is his longing for the spiritual divine that he is forced to conquer those very instincts in some way.

His first volume R e d e m p t i o n s (E r l ö s u n g e n) represents this struggle between matter and spirit: with a pathos and sway of rhythm which occasionally remind of Schiller, with a bluntness, here and there, which is Heine's. As Schiller found a solution of the conflict in the neutrality of play, in the esthetic sense, in the enfranchisement of our actions from relative purposes, so Dehmel in the negation of ulterior aims. "So soon as spirit knows of nothing else but its instincts, there will be revealed to it the essential wisdom of amorous folly and the Great Love." Demonic lusts as well as harmless courting or any assertion of life, are sanctified by a realization of the inner connection of all existence. Even a grimace proves the god whom it distarts. And even the purest in heart will, within the turmoil of temptations, have the experience that the spirit's true strivings are tested by aberrations. The prayer "Lead us not into temptation" Dehmel emphatically opposes by "Lead us into temptation".

The Great Love — as defined in subsequent books —

is the continuous interrelation between universe and individual. Whoever has possessed himself of this love and is fully conscious of it, is superior to all temporal ethics. He is capable of acting harmoniously; he has awakened in him God, in as much as he no longer uses the standard of a transient Good or Evil but the standard of life's eternal values. Accordingly each individual must be his own saviour, may attain perfect beatitude in this world. The universe does not grant only one redemption to all, but rather a thousand redemptions to every single individual: "whatever delights, terrifies, shocks man, that redeems him, since it expands him and fills him with life".

Needless to say that this principle of dynamic ethics or of non-morality is Nietzsche's bequest whose disciple Dehmel reverently declares himself. He differs, however, from Nietzsche in his belief that perfect happiness is not only worth striving for but really possible, now, at any time. It is not our generation's mission to contribute its small share to the evolution of the future superman. Our generation, as any, is an end in itself, the superman, "God", being inherent in every human being. Nietzsche's philosophy is consistently dynamic, regardless of the individual's happiness. Dehmel's philosophy is dynamic only with reference to the individual's relations to his neighbors; it is hedonistic as far as the individual's own existence is concerned. Since any increase of personal bliss means g o o d, any decrease e v i l, the law of g o o d a n d e v i l, collectively discarded, remains the moral standard individually. Since what is evil for others may be good for me,

and vice versa, this whole philosophy is untenable as a
system, applicable only — perhaps — in the one case of
its originator. It is a subjective phantasm, a self-redemp-
tion at best, not a gospel for others.

Mystics of all ages consider sexual love a symbol of
the ultimate harmony of individual and cosmic consciousness. Quite so Dehmel. The union of man and wife is
identical in essence with the union of all creation. He who
has once enjoyed the unrestrained bliss of such a union,
realizing its eternal significance, has completed the course
of his existence. Universal love, as pure contemplation,
is in itself not active. It is not necessarily put into practice
with regard to one's fellow-beings. However, the abstract
mystery of love may be supplemented by the involuntary-
voluntary phenomenon of concrete propagation, by the
relation of creator and creature. The group of mother and
child which, in varying illumination, appears over and
over again, is the symbol of unselfish love, of active sympathy. According to the belief that a thousand redemptions
are possible for every individual, the Holy Virgin is not
the only chosen one. Any mother may give birth to a
saviour: at least to a saviour for herself. On the other
hand, a mother's unselfish love redeems her child from
sin. All the tormenting longings of an erring son vanish
at a glance of motherly eyes. The books L o v e ' s
C h a o s (A b e r d i e L i e b e) and W o m a n a n d
W o r l d (W e i b u n d W e l t) lead up to this view. An
additional volume T h e T r a n s f o r m a t i o n s o f V e -
n u s (D i e V e r w a n d l u n g e n d e r V e n u s) treats

of the erotic problem as such in form of rhapsodies that reach from V e n u s R e l i g i o s a down to V e n u s P e r v e r s a, exhausting their theme with a boldness and directness unequalled even by Walt Whitman. The pantomime L u c i f e r also belongs in this connection.

We need not be surprised at strange contradictions in an artist. Dehmel, a son of bourgeois parents, unlike aristocratic Liliencron, sympathized, far more intensively than he with the woes of the common people. His collectivistic instinct, irreconcilable as it is with his egotistic ethics, would have led him to socialistic poems, if he never had developed that mystic theory referred to. One of this group T h e W o r k m a n (D e r A r b e i t s m a n n) is as great as any ever produced in this field. It is neither a home nor the daily necessities of life that the laborer misses, but t i m e to enjoy all that is created by the work of his hands. In plain, yet suggestive, imagery here one of the most difficult problems of our civilization has found expression. Social love in its sublime grandeur is glorified in P r o m e t h e u s U n b o u n d (D e r b e f r e i t e P r o - m e t h e u s). Prometheus, released at last after ages of torture, descends from the mountain to his beloved mortals to see the blessings which his sacrifice had wrested from the gods. He finds material progress and prosperity all over the world but the character of man unchanged: hatred and strife as before, nay even a new vice formerly unknown- envy. Is this disgusting sight meant to be a more cruel punishment than the first one thought out for him by wily Zeus? The Titan, seized with despair and wrath, begins to destroy the cultivated fields and fine homesteads around him, when he is halted by a thrilling event. Two men, hitherto bitter enemies, forget their hatred in fighting for their lives against the raging elements, rescue each other, and fall into a loving embrace. Now Prometheus believes in his mission once more. He sends a joyful prayer of thanks up to Zeus,: the love of those two men alone outweighs the evils of the world and his own sufferings.

Free from premeditation, the natural results of instinctive impulses are the actions of naive children. Dehmel, the meditating godseeker, the problematical artist, longs for the paradise of childhood. Alone, as well as in cooperation with his first wife, he composed a large number of poems and short stories for children. He considered this so important a part of his work that he enclosed among his collected writings a separate volume: K i n d e r - g a r t e n. A comparison with Stevenson suggests itself all the more readily since the K i n d e r g a r t e n contains an excellent translation of T h e L a n d o f C o u n t e r - p a n e under the title D e r k l e i n e L a z a r u s. On the whole it may be said that A C h i l d ' s G a r d e n of V e r s e s is more genuinely childlike than Dehmel's book. On the other hand the grown-up reader will find a greater variety of genuine poetry in the latter. Dehmel's rhythm is too personally weighty; his thoughts are, in a majority of cases, too complex for the purpose. Stevenson's vocabulary and idea's too, sometimes go beyond a child's capacity, but the melodious rhythm, the easy flow of his verses, as a rule bring about a spontaneous contact with the child's soul. However, these are reflections of a grown person. The children of the present writer are able to enjoy both books and they do not seem to have a pronounced predilection for either one of them.

II.

Dehmel, declaring love the solution of the great world-riddle, does not say anything new. He simply gives another version to the principle doctrine of the Christian gospel. Indeed, Richard Schaukal, probably the most sensitive and intelligent of the poet's critics, justly remarks that Dehmel, in spite of all his seemingly ultra-modern philosophizing, is irresistibly drawn toward Christ. It is not impossible that he will sometime return to the conservative faith of his fathers: if he can eliminate from his philosophy its anarchistic elements; if he comes to realize the practical consequences of that ideal of self-control which he, like Liliencron, demands. His greatest and most ambitious work M a n a n d W o m a n (Z w e i M e n - s c h e n) leaves this an open question.

He calls it a "novel in ballads" ("Roman in Romanzen") and expresses his conviction of having created in it the form of modern epic. — His books of poetry, in their final version, are all divided into groups according to a definite plan. They read like cycles, conceived as such from the beginning. Those of the poems that are below the author's own average, singly, gain in power, standing out effectively against the background of a compact unit. The very best, however, lose that organic independence which gives the pure l y r i c its aerial buoyancy. They must be taken out from the barriers of the system in order to be fully valued. What Dr. Bertz said of L e a v e s o f G r a s s is true of Dehmel's poetry: the parts are greater than the whole. Selections like the one published by Dehmel himself or as in Vesper's D i e E r n t e reveal an astounding wealth of lyric marvels. The books in their entirety are monotonous as to their form, irritatingly contradictory as to their contents. They seem too artificially constructed. Most of this may be said of Z w e i M e n s c h e n.

We admire the immense will-power involved in creating a connected series of faultlessly rimed poems which group themselves with mathematical exactness into three chapters of 36 ballads each, each again of 36 lines. But to be an epos the content is too abstract. To be a lyric there is, here, too close an interrelation between the constituent parts. Only a few will bear separation from their environment. The work, then, belongs to that unfortunate class of hybrids, so frequently produced by romantic artists, which are condemned to pendulate forever between life and death.

A man, Lukas, and a woman, Lea, are elective affinities but each bound by legal ties. Both shake off their fetters. Lea deserts her husband and poisons her blind child, thereby removing even the last external obstacle between herself and Lukas. He leaves his wife who dies from grief. Both struggle for some time with pangs of conscience but finally absolve themselves mutually from guilt. For they acted, as they come to be convinced, prompted by a spirit whose only aim is the peace of clarity.

Stronger yet than this external obstacle is an internal one. Lukas demands of woman — everything is typical, symbolical — perfect surrender, unhesitating veracity and frankness, absolute naturalness, physical as well as spiritual, ready disclosure of all weaknesses great or small. Lea insists that she is what he thinks her to be. Man's illusionary ideal of woman must not be destroyed. That is to say: he desires objective essence of character, she subjective appearance. Lea yields. At the close of the first cycle — Knowledge (Die Erkenntnis) — both, in their bodily union, anticipate true happiness. In the second cycle — Beatitude (Die Seligkeit) they attain also the communion of souls and therewith the highest degree of individual bliss; they divine the bliss of the world in their own. In the third cycle — Clarity (Die Klarheit) — they reach the bliss of collective love. They perceive that their individual experience is only a symbol of universal life. They have passed through Good and Evil, Heaven and Hell, unscathed. They have remained true to themselves and to each other. They have spiritualized, sanctified, their animal-human instincts by asserting, not by denying them. They have reached the ideal of divine humanity by their union of perfect manhood and womanhood. And by their example they have shown others the way to the same ideal. In this sense, indeed, their salvation is the world's salvation.

Lukas, having taken part in nihilistic intrigues, is exiled. Instead of Lea going with him as she could, since they are materially independent, they agree to separate for ever. The consciousness of the universality of their love will keep them united in all eternity. And this consciousness can evince its vital power of unselfishness only by an actual separation of their physical existence.

These ideas are but another proof of the old experience that all attempts to replace the Christian ethics by new systems easily lead to anarchism. That dual beatitude, that world-salvation rests upon a crumbling foundation. It is true, the lovers do feel compunctions as to their guilt. But the absolution they find is so complete, their atonement so conveniently in the line of their desires that, by an insensible turn, sin becomes virtue. It is their very guilt that enriches their lives and leads them on to their realization of cosmic bliss. It never occurs to them that they might reach their ultimate destination by individual self-renunciation and fulfillment of their duties, nor that universal sympathy first of all means a respect for the unquestionable rights of others. As it is, even the unnecessary, the murder of the child, appears to them as an act of metaphysical necessity. A victorious general too, they agree, under whose command thousands die for the benefit of others, would prefer to spare the lives of his soldiers, if he only could. This is metaphysical sophistry.

Dehmel, the prophet, then, is at least as problematical as Nietzsche. What will last of his Zwei Menschen is not the philosophy underlying but the esthetic beauty

of many of the ballads. The intimate harmony of nature
and man in these poems is magnificent. Every single one
begins with a graphic sketch of the surrounding landscape
and its pacticular mood. In every single case we have the
convincing impression of universal connections. There are
no repetitions. More than a hundred different scenes, and
each with a distinctive character of its own subtly yet
clearly brought out. There are abysses of melancholy and
despair as terrifying, heights of exuberant joy as enrapturing as in any poetry; a dazzling display of imaginative
and creative faculty worthy of the greatest masters. Likewise the metrical structure is admirable. The ballads are
not arranged in strophes but follow a rhythm free enough
to express every shade of feeling, regular enough to maintain throughout the series a uniformity of motion. All in
all Z w e i M e n s c h e n, as to its details, is an artistic
achievement of exceptionally high order which would have
deserved a less problematical content.

Dehmel's only drama *) so far is T h e F e l l o w - M a n
(D e r M i t m e n s c h) and based upon the same moral
principles as Z w e i M e n s c h e n. A theoretical intro-
duction purports to show that tragedy is no longer to be
considered the highest form of art. Our philosophical and
religious ideas have completely changed. We do not believe in a transcendental God nor in a permanently established moral law. On the contrary, we believe that the
divine is immanent in every part of the world, that all
existence is identically one, that this One is undergoing an

---

*) A new tragi-comedy has just appeared: "Michel Michael".

eternal evolution. Consequently there is no moral law, but a progressive crystallization of ethics effected by an interchange of uncontrollable forces. In this evolution every single manifestation of will-power is a co-operative factor. "This makes it psychologically impossible for us to attribute to the physical destruction of personal energy as immense an importance as the most impressive representation of tragic fate demands." The ideal, then, is a tragicomedy like Shakespeare's T r o i l u s   a n d   C r e s - s i d a , i. e., a drama which expresses an ironical philosophy superior to the joys and sorrows of individual man.

In objection to this theory we must say that Shakespeare himself left a much larger number of pure tragedies. They were, indeed, born from that Christian transcendentalism which Dehmel condemns. But the old Christian faith is certainly no more afraid of death than is the new monistic theory: "Death, where is thy sting, Grave, where is thy victory?" Shakespeare, as well as Corneille and Racine and Schiller, found death a tragic phenomenon in as much as it definitely cuts short individual existence and volition for this life, although the life beyond must have seemed to them immeasurably more important. Is not every Christian impressed by the tragic awe of Gethsemane and Golgatha, in spite of his anticipating the resurrection?

There is no reason, then, why genuine tragedy should no longer be possible under the modern religion of an optimistically tinged monism. Moreover, even "strictly scientific" monism may have a pessimistic tendency from the view-point of the individual. This whole question is decided from case to case by temperament rather than by logic. Lastly, any shade of modern monism is as yet a hypothesis which may appeal to the intellect of a few, not a general faith. In order to become a civilizing and cultural power like Christianity, Monism will have to make its abstract theory a concrete image, will have to create a new mythology. Not until then it can replace the old faith or produce a new class of literature in Dehmel's sense. Richard Wagner's chaotic constructions show how futile individual attempts at forestalling new mythologies must be.

If the poet succeeds in forcing us into his point of view within the frame of his work, we do not care about the metaphysical truth of his philosophy. Ibsen's G h o s t s , based upon a doubtful theory of heredity, is esthetically convincing, because the d r a m a t i s p e r - s o n a e are human beings of flesh and blood, and because they do believe in the inevitableness of heredity. The motivation, therefore, is so completely logical that there is no room for doubt. We leave the theater with the over-whelming impression of gigantic fate, no matter whether we are Christians, or Jews, Dualists, or Monists.

Dehmel's drama neither fulfils his own demands nor the demands of any other system, philosophical or esthetic. — The brothers Ernst and Peter Wächter live together. Peter is a talented architect who has made an invention that is to be exploited by a company of capitalists. One of these is Nathan. Nathan's beautiful daughter Thora is engaged to his partner Eickrott whom she has learned to despise as a brutal roué. She meets Peter, is seized by passionate love, and gives herself to him. Ernst, the fellow-man, possessing no creative power himself, has made it the mission of his life to be the helpmate of his brother. The latter is to reach the highest possible perfection in his art. This can be accomplished only by absolute concentration. Peter is not intended for love and matrimony, Ernst thinks. So he does all he can to separate his brother from Thora. With an astonishingly ingenious cruelty he persuades Thora that she will make Peter unhappy. Not wishing to become Eickrott's prey, she commits suicide, proving thereby that she was under-estimated by Ernst. Eickrott, now finding out the truth, challenges Peter to a pistol-duel. Presenting his challenge personally he grossly insults his rival and is knocked unconscious and partially blinded by a blow of Peter's fist. Ernst now insists upon taking the entire responsibility upon his shoulders, since Peter's art, the greater value, is necessary to the world. Peter, refusing to accept such a sacrifice is prevailed upon by Ernst to summon a physician. In his absence Ernst shoots Eickrott dead, fully conscious of what such a deed means. He, the inactive and useless one, goes to jail. Peter will remain free, his art, the higher value, will be triumphant, now that Eickrott, the last obstacle, has been removed. The murder was committed "in the name of God".

In his preface Dehmel has the following to say: "The fatalistic drama D e r M i t m e n s c h has been changed into a tragicomedy, where the problematical tendency is superseded by the impulsive conflict and which perhaps now, at last, will be understood by managers of theaters." This is a mistake. The more intensely this play is studied, the less intelligible become its action and characters, the more painfully evident becomes the inconsistency of motivation. There is no central will-conflict at all. Peter and Thora are played by Ernst like the men in a game of chess. Ernst is not a human being, but a puppet arbitrarily set in motion by the author. By what right does Ernst assume his dictatorial guardianship over his brother? How does he know that Thora will be Peter's ruin? Is he unaware of the fact that great love-passions have stimulated geniuses to their most perfect works? Is a woman who is strong enough to die for a man too weak to live for him? And how about Peter's duty after he has once enjoyed Thora's love? Even her death is unable to bring that reckoning-machine called Ernst to his senses. He continues to play the rôle of Providence. He decrees that the world's welfare makes another murder necessary, that Peter's future achievements will fully compensate for both. He is omniscient. He believes that he is inaugurating a higher moral standard in the name of God, while he returns to the feudal club-law. With a view toward eternity he believes that he is doing his duty as the martyr of an ideal, while he neglects his real duties in the present, and becomes the martyr only of an illusion which, if general, would annihilate human society.

If this play possessed the convincing vitality of Shakespeare or the fascinating pathos of Schiller, it would have to be designated as one of the most dangerous documents of social revolution. But there is no real life in it. It is a philosophical construction, the ultra-subjective solution of a self-proposed problem. In this sense, to be sure, we cannot take the catastrophe seriously. And we should have to ask the question, whether the poet did not, in the last analysis, intend to make fun of his readers, if he had not expounded, with unmistakable seriousness, the same anarchistic principles in Z w e i M e n s c h e n and other poems.

Neither the lyrical epicist, nor the dramatist, nor the thinker and prophet seems to hold an unassailable position. In the writer's opinion only Dehmel's lyrics will remain a permanent asset of literature, as far as his contradictory, chimaera-like genius has granted him pure lyrics.

He compares himself with those ponderous birds of prey that rise with difficulty but, once in the air, soar with a free and easy and steady swing. If he had been a less genuine artist he would have followed the line of least resistance. But there was no task too great for him to attack. If he failed in his struggle for a new religion, the struggle itself was worth while; and Dehmel's stupendous energy displayed in it commands our respect. The artistic side of the problem he overcame as well as any of his predecessors, i. e. to give the process of philosophical thinking concrete form by raising it to the level of passionate feeling. He lacks only Schiller's consistency to deserve a place beside him as a philosophical poet.

Fortunately Dehmel's soul is such a spacious organism that a part of it is capable of the most variegated emotional experiences without being affected by abstract reasoning.

He does know how to rise and soar. And he is still in the prime of his life; he is such a deep, inexhaustible character, such an incessant worker that it is impossible for us to see, how far and high the wings of his genius will yet take him.

*　　*

*

It is not a bad omen for Dehmel that in his romantic quest of the blue flower he always found the way back again to reality. It was left to a younger man to carry Dehmel's cosmic symbolism to an extreme. A l f r e d M o m b e r t (b. 1872), as no one else in our age, is the romanticist p a r e x c e l l e n c e. He is Hardenberg and Whitman combined. He attempts to create single-handed a new mythology of limitless dimensious. He is, in the widest sense of Fichte's ego-centric subjectivism, the master of the universe. Day and night and the seasons, man and nature, lands and oceans, stars and moons and suns, and the infinite spaces of nothingness are all interlocked in one great harmony. The poet's task is not only to find the ultimate One, the final Only, the Eternal, but to generate and produce it by his own creative will. His task is "to concentrate the universe with all its planets, suns, and infinities into one formula of emotion." Symbols thereby are made symbols of symbols. Mombert sings, e. g., the ecstatic love of man for woman. But the woman's shimmering body is suddenly transformed into a sun; her long flowing hair are rays pouring their light over the man. The sun is the creator of all life in this visible world.

6*

But this sun of ours is only a symbol of other, greater, primeval suns, of transcendental worlds. Or woman is the personification of the sea, the sea in its turn the symbol of eternity.

The book A - G l o w (D e r G l ü h e n d e) represents man as freed from the shackles of physical existence and penetrating to eternal perceptions by force of spiritual intuition: the delirious visions of fever. In C r e a t i o n (Die Schöpfung) the poet experiences the god-like ecstasy of creating a world, the sensation of being God: the hallucinations of insanity. In another volume T h e T h i n k e r (D e r D e n k e r) the instinct of creating power is supplemented by λόγος, the organizing intellect. T h e B l o s s o m o f C h a o s (D i e B l ü t e d e s C h a o s), T h e S u n - S p i r i t (D e r S o n n e g e i s t), the "symphonic drama" A e o n , t h e W o r l d ' s F u l f i l l m e n t (A e o n d e r W e l t g e s u c h t e), and the selection T h e H e a v e n l y D r i n k e r (D e r H i m m l i s c h e Z e c h e r) are the titles of Mombert's further works.

It would be a futile undertaking to attempt an analysis of their contents. There is no concreteness of images. It is all one intangible metaphysical vagueness. A fervid longing for immeasurable spaces far beyond any known stellar systems; that longing's superhumanly creative power, unfathomable depth and torturing pain; the dull tension of expectation before, the overflowing joy of success after complete communion with the universe is reached; the bold, defiant heroism of struggle, the sublime consciousness, the lordly pride of divinity attained: such transcendent emotions Mombert puts into words. And, incredible as it seems, these aetherial, mystic feelings, this abstract abandon, is expressed almost as perfectly as if it were effected by music, the metaphysical art proper. Mombert's attitude toward things is the attitude of a musician. His language is the completion of Novalis' ideal. It possesses an equally full sonority and surpasses it by a subtly suggestive, divinatory force, a tender flexibility, a sweet gracefulness, a magnetic cohesiveness beyond anything written by the first romanticists. This his enrichment of the language of his nation is in itself an achievement of no small importance for the future. Mombert's theosophical flights, however, are the extreme stages of mystic romanticism. Here is the boundary where the possibilities of human experience, intuitive or intellctual, where the possibilities of expression end, where the land of insanity, chaos begins. It is to be hoped that Mombert, like Dehmel, becomes aware of this danger. It would be an irreparable loss to literature to have this great talent go the way of Hölderlin and Nietzsche.

IV.

Gerhart Hauptmann

———

Silesian farmlands were found to contain an abundance
of coal. Plain peasants over night become wealthy capitalists who, exempt from labor, do not know what to do
with their time. Idleness is the parent of vice. For the
peasants there exist no higher enjoyments than eating,
drinking, and what they understand by "love". They degenerate rapidly in a slough of coarse passions. Greed,
alcohol, lewdness are their atmosphere and horizon. In the
house of the Krauses these vices have reached the stage of
indescribable monstrosity. Only Helene, Krause's daughter
by his first wife who died young, has remained pure.
Having been born before the corruption set in, she received, by the will of her mother, a good moral education in
a boarding-school of the Moravian Brotherhood. Ever
since her return home she has longed for a life far away
from this terrible environment, for a life among people
who are human beings, no brutes.

Loth, a young idealist, a socialistic agitator, suddenly
enters this circle. He wishes to study the situation of the
miners. For here as everywhere they are the victims of
shameless exploitation: Helene and Loth love each other
at first sight. A heavenly idyl in a hell of crime. Helene's
fervid yearning for purity and bliss will be fulfilled. Loth

will take her with him as his wife. He is faithful and true,
a champion of social sympathy and responsibility. And
no tie binds Helene to her family which long has ceased to
be a human organization. She is of age and the independent owner of her mother's heritage.

She is mistaken. Loth is anything but what he appeared to be and what he really was. Or rather, the real Loth
is replaced by a paper-dummy representing some abstract
theories as e. g. the law of heredity, total abstinence, sexual
hygiene, eugenics. Loth is told by a country-doctor that
the Krause family is afflicted with hereditary dipsomania.
He consequently considers it his duty to posterity not to
raise any weakminded children such as Helene might bear
him, although she does not drink herself and although it
is doubtful whether her father was a drunkard before she
was born. Precaution is for Loth the better part of sympathy and decency. A discussion with Helene would be
somewhat embarrassing. A written note answers the purpose as well. Loth disappears from the scene. Helene
forgetting in her grief that even without Loth she is free
to go wherever she pleases, kills herself in order not to
fall a prey to her brutish relatives.

This is the plot of Gerhart Hauptmann's first play
B e f o r e S u n r i s e (V o r S o n n e n a u f g a n g) which
in 1889 was performed by the Berlin Théatre Libre ("Freie
Bühne") under sensational circumstances. Naturalism
which in the lyric and in the novel had already become
a determining influence, seemed now to have taken posses-

sion of the theater also. Hauptmann was hailed by many
as the chosen leader to an entirely new kind of drama.

However, there was nothing absolutely new in B e -
f o r e S u n r i s e. The crassness of the subject was no
greater than in certain productions of the "storm and
stress" period a hundred and twenty years before. The
vividness of characterization was no greater than in Bjarne
Holmsen's P a p a H a m l e t, Hauptmann's model. The
law of heredity, the results of alcoholism had been depicted
more forcibly and more convincingly by Ibsen in G h o s t s,
by Tolstoy in T h e P o w e r o f D a r k n e s s. Zola's
L a T e r r e had exhausted the possibilities of disgusting
brutality to the extreme. B e f o r e S u n r i s e was rela-
tively new for the German theater in as much as, since
Hebbel's and Ludwig's death, the public had more and more
become accustomed to the superficialities incessantly imported from Paris by Paul Lindau and other literary business men. It was for this reason chiefly that the philistines,
high and low, felt shocked at the ghastly reflex of darkest
Germany.

There was no indication of talent in the construction
of the plot. This is, as in nearly all of Hauptmann's
successive plays, an epic story developed in dialogform and
in itself lacking the necessary strictness of motivation.
What then and later attracted the best judges were rather
the personal qualities of the author. In the midst of the
crudities of subject-matter there were embedded a strangely
fascinating simplicity and fervor of feeling, a touching love
for the poor and lowly, a sweet fragrance of nature-scenes:

merits that pointed to a genuine, if somewhat narrow and lyrically tempered, talent for narration.

New for the stage was the finely individualizing gradation of speech from the conventional High German of the "cultured" down to the broad provincialisms of the laborers, from the stuttering and horse-like neighing of the drunkard up to the soft whisper of first love.

The hero is as little consistent as the plot. Loth is not to appear as a dishonest and fickleminded person from the beginning. On the contrary: the author does everything to characterize him as a noble friend of the people, as a model of honesty. But at the end he acts so completely in contradiction to himself that it would necessitate a long and psychologically intelligible process of transformation in order to make the beginning and the end of his career seem to harmonize. Othello, in murdering Desdemona, is essentially the same man as when we first meet him. The Loth of the fifth act shares only his name with the Loth of the first. This inconsistency of character-drawing permanently remained one of Hauptmann's principal weaknesses. Likewise portentous for his future was the over-abundance of talking at the expense of dramatic progress. A central will-conflict, the soul of dramatic action, is absent here as in most of the following plays. Helene is in no sense a heroine; she merely accepts what is allotted to her. However, passive as her longing for salvation is, it could have been made in Loth the cause of an inner struggle and the incentive for action, if he were more than a mechanical compilation of formulas.

Loth repeatedly discusses the relation between employers and employées, the adjustment of labor and wages. This innermost problem of economic evolution, only talked of in B e f o r e S u n r i s e was visualized three years later in concrete images. Coal-miners changed places with weavers.

The Weavers.

About the middle of the nineteenth century, when socialism first became a vital factor in Germany, Heine wrote his terrible song of the Silesian weavers who sit at their looms gnashing their teeth, weaving Germany's shroud, and weaving into it a threefold curse. In his poem F r o m t h e S i l e s i a n M o u n t a i n s Freiligrath had the same people in view. Hauptmann's father had been one of those victims of capitalistic exploitation. The memory of that gloomy time was kept alive in the family, and the poet himself always remained in contact with his native province where conditions are not much better to-day than they were in 1844.

The Silesian weavers did not rise in revolt against the state in order to put into practice the radical demands of liberty, equality, fraternity. What they wanted was literally this: to have a square-meal for once, to have a breath of fresh air for once, to feel like human beings for once. They troop together, drive away their most hated oppressor, and, in the intoxication of a collective power never before experienced, they demolish a few buildings. After a brief local success they are "brought to their senses" again by a few shots of a company of soldiers. Their misery is as great as ever. They continue to starve. Their oppressors return and soon recover their losses. This historic event (according to Paul Schlenther) is, in the main, the plot of the drama.

Its hero is the wretched, down-trodden weaver-population; its all-compelling fate, starvation. One picture of misery follows another in quick succession; dozens of types of decay drawn with marvelous truthfulness. All grades of generations and view-points, from the paltry remainders of a better past to the youngest, saddest martyrs of the desperate present. All resembling one another in their humbleness, their weakness, their patience, their longing. The most industrious, loyal, innocent people drained to the last drop by the vampire of capitalism. State and church, in Mammon's service, conspiring against the poorest of the poor. Nobles, citizens, peasants, their oppressors or exploiters. A small number of intelligent sympathizers.

The weavers have no leader to save them. Only one or two young fellows who happened to spend some time outside their own community, who have physical strength enough left in them to come to a decision, dare express what all have felt so long. At last, after years of mute suffering their latent anger finds an outlet. They take courage to mention an old song against their tyrants. The song is next recited, then sung by a few, finally by all as a war-cry. The revolt is under way, spreads from village to village, culminates in a temporary success. But the soldiers will return to quench for ever the flickering flame.

In this drama Hauptmann created a truly naturalistic work of art. The germ of his esthetic experience was fully developed to maturity without the slightest interference of momentary, subjectively idealizing moods. (He succeeded in identifying himself so objectively with each and every *EXPRESSION* one of his characters as to give each its own individual life. Nowhere does the author's person intrude. Each individual within his peculiar aura shares the atmosphere of the entirety. The reality of the given part of nature is transfused into the form of art as completely as imaginable.)

Dazzled at first by the glaring directness, bewildered by the opalescent diversity of life, we soon are irresistibly drawn into the one emotion common to all. We need not endeavor to convince ourselves of the truth of this or that phenomenon. It is all a vital experience of our own heart. In spite of the great complexity of the scenic events there is no relaxation of the dramatic tension. Slowly but steadily the action rises to the end which brings climax and catastrophe together. The dramatic action here for once consists in the awakening, extension, and concentric transmission of positive energy from a few to the masses.

In the conventional sense of the word the weaver-drama is not tragic. The misery of starvation does not have its cause in the character of the victim. There is, then, no absolute necessity of fate. But the relative necessity of this typical case seems tragic enough, i. e. the fact that, in the midst of a so-called Christian civilization, there are always men who make their neighbors starve, while they revel in luxury themselves. Tragic it is that the egotistic instinct of man seems eternally superior to his altruistic theory. The theme of the play is not, as has been asserted: "there must be higher wages" but: "is there justice on earth?" The poet believes not. His No is not a violation of esthetic canons as some critics would have it. His Yes would have been a moral untruth. And this is the guilt of mankind. T h e W e a v e r s is more than an accusation against an exceptional or transient case of human organization. It is the severe but just condemnation of an entire system which, in two thousand years, failed to put into practice the highest command of The Saviour.

*   *

*

There are artists who, carried along by a powerful movement, privileged by a happy mood of creative Nature, occasionally reach a plane far above their average ability. None of Hauptmann's former or later plays can compare with T h e W e a v e r s. His name, so it appears to us today, will go down to posterity as the author of T h e W e a v e r s.

As "Social Dramas" he classifies with the two already discussed the "thieves' comedy", T h e B e a v e r - c a p e and its sequel, the "tragi-comedy" T h e R e d C o c k (D e r B i b e r p e l z 1893; D e r r o t e H a h n 1901). Both plays treat of the social question in this respect: first, the detection of crimes is prevented largely in consequence of the judge's prejudice against witnesses who are political suspects; second, the chief characters belong to the lowest stratum of the population. In the former play Frau Wolff has stolen a valuable beaver-cape. Everybody knows that she is the thief, except the stupid judge Wehrhahn who praises her, the faithful laundress of his house, as a model of bourgeois virtue. In the latter play Frau Wolff, widowed, has married a police-spy by the name of Fielitz. Judge Wehrhahn is as stupid as ever. So Frau Wolff-Fielitz ventures to set fire to her shanty after heavily insuring it. Insurance Company and judge alike allow themselves to be duped and enable the incendiary to build a handsome new house. This is the comical part. When the house is near completion the heroine dies of heart-failure. This is the tragic counter-part. In both cases the subject was just about weighty enough for a funny grotesque. Hauptmann did not even reach this level, for, making the judge so impossibly stupid he dissolves the comical elements of the plot into empty aimlessness.

Naturalistic as to their technique, "social" as to their environment are C a r r i e r H e n s c h e l (F u h r m a n n H e n s c h e l 1898) and R o s e B e r n d (1903). A man of strong physique, good heart, and limited intellect, promises his dying wife that he will never marry the servant girl Hanne, a young woman of dangerously sensual temperament. He breaks his promise, because he needs an efficient housekeeper and because he is unconsciously fascinated by Hanne's crude animality. He discovers himself to be deceived by her, finds in his disgrace a just punishment for his breach of promise, and commits suicide. — The nucleus of this play is a short story R a i l r o a d - g u a r d T h i e l of 1887 written in the style of Zola.

R o s e B e r n d is the tragedy of a beautiful country-girl who is driven to sin and crime by the unscrupulous voluptuousness of men.

Both works vividly picture their respective environ-ment. But the motivation is extremely weak. The decisive events, which call for a creative faculty of the highest order, are cautiously made to take place between acts. Conse-quently their results, when discussed on the stage, do not have the convincing effect desired.

* *
*

The same thing is true of F l o r i a n G e y e r, "the tragedy of the peasant-war". It is a social drama like T h e W e a v e r s and ought to bear the title T h e P e a s a n t s. The principle theme is identical: the revolt of a barbarously enslaved estate against their tyrants; the attempt of the German peasants in the first quarter of the sixteenth cen-tury to force justice from the feudal nobility, after all complaints had been ignored. There is again no central hero. It is true, the peasants have a leader, the former knight Florian Geyer who joined them, in spite of his rank, out of unselfish sympathy. He is a valiant warrior, a pru-dent general. But he does not succeed in overcoming the distrust of the masses or the envy of his peasant rivals for leadership. It is comparatively few that follow him, and the decisive struggle occurs in his absence, against his commands. He himself and the peasants perish because he was not obeyed. His fate is the tragedy of futile self-sacrifice; the fate of the peasants the tragedy of extravagance in times of success, of disunion and waste of energy, of shortsightedness in times of crises.

In contrast to T h e W e a v e r s we do not here see the genesis and growth of the revolt. The pre-suppositions are awkwardly communicated to the spectator by means of an old-fashioned prelude which consists largely of reading from a written document. The drama proper does not contain the important actions but rather the reports of what has happened and the impressions of these reports upon the audience. We get acquainted with innumerable characters. They, together with the reports of events, enable us to imagine somewhat vaguely the actual tragedy behind the scenes. This method of indirectness, so contrary to all dramatic principles, caused the utter failure of the play when first put on the stage in Berlin (1896).

Since the representatives of the counter-plot are generally only spoken of, there is no dramatic tension at all and no possibility of judging as to whether or not the nominal hero Florian Geyer was a hero indeed. That he can die like a man — so much we see in the very last scene after the horrible annihilation of his wretched associates.

If the work is not a good drama, it might still be a powerful epos in the form of dialog. But even if viewed from this standpoint, it does not fulfil a high artistic ideal. An epicist, too, must not avoid visual representation of essential events. Homer would not be Homer, if he had only given a colorless report from hearsay of Odysseus' battle with the suitors instead of depicting the battle directly.

Florian Geyer, then, one of Hauptmann's most ambitious and most elaborate works is of no enduring value beyond being another expression of a pure, noble, and sympathetic heart. From amidst the coarseness and atrocity of feudalism shines forth the ardent hope for the abolition of social discriminations, for the recognition of individual rights, for that kingdom of justice, of love, of liberty, the enticing mirage of which Luther's reformation had conjured up, and for which the time was not — is not — yet ripe.

II.

Under the title "Family Dramas" Hauptmann comprises four plays that deal with the life of the middle-classes. The first one, The Peace-Festival (Das Friedensfest, 1890), treats of a similar problem as Before Sunrise, its immediate predecessor: the decay of a family, caused here by nervous prostration of both parents, a hereditary malady which, with the father, leads to mania of persecution, with the children to paralyzing pessimism. The relation of Loth to Helene is reversed. One of the sons, Wilhelm, is to be saved by his strong-minded fiancée Ida from the demons of the parental home. The play, a marked advance upon the former, represents a real conflict of wills, i. e. Ida's tenacious fight for her own and Wilhelm's happiness, and Wilhelm's struggle with his inherited disease which, temporarily checked, breaks out with ever renewed force after his return home. The suppositions point to a tragic end. The woman, Ida, to be sure, steadfastly clings to her lover, never giving up her fight — a significant contrast to the "man" Loth. But Wilhelm seems to be hopelessly crushed by the family demon. And yet, after closely following Ibsen's G h o s t s, Hauptmann deviates from his model when it comes to drawing the consequences from the situation. It seems, as though the author, out of love for his characters, had been reluctant to bring the catastrophe upon them. On the other hand, he did not quite believe in the possibility of complete salvation. So he makes his fine psychological study end with an unsatisfactory compromise, with a question to the future.

The next play L o n e l y P e o p l e (E i n s a m e M e n - s c h e n, 1891) is hardly more than a version of Ibsen's R o s m e r s h o l m in a more realistic form. Johannes Vockerath is introduced as a man of genius, bound to an insignificant wife who is unable to understand his work. The son of orthodox parents, he has liberal ideas without freeing himself from conventional ethics entirely. He finds an affinity in the Russian student Anna Mahr. Neither radical enough to leave his wife and to follow Anna, nor strong enough to live without the only friend he has ever found, he kills himself as did Helene.

The poet does not succeed in convincing us of the seriousness of the situation. Johannes is by no means the great genius which he thinks himself to be, which the author intended him to be. He is writing a revolutionary book, as he assures us, but throughout the whole play he does not utter a word that goes beyond the horizon of an average intellect. His wife seems rather superior to him than otherwise. The question, then, seems justified, if it is not this very self-conceit that causes the tragedy. But such was not the author's intention. Johannes is indeed supposed to be the unappreciated genius. Likewise Fräulein Mahr is represented to be a type of the perfect woman of the twentieth century: a combination of spiritual culture and those virtues that have always been considered peculiar to woman. As a matter of fact she is certainly no better, perhaps worse than the average of her sex. Intellectually she does not appear Frau Vockerath's superior; morally she is her inferior. From the very beginning she displays an amazing lack of thoughtfulness and her brazen defiance of the laws of hospitality is more than incredibly shameless.

A glance at R o s m e r s h o l m suffices to show the superficiality of plot and composition in its German parallel. In the former every word spoken, even by minor characters, has a direct bearing upon the dramatic conflict pressing it on toward the catastrophe. Rebekka and Rosmer are completely what the author means them to be. They as well as Beate are deep, passionate natures whose interrelations cannot but evolve the dreadful crisis the drama represents. We believe in Rosmer's ideal of "Adelsmenschen", since we see him approach his ideal himself and unconsciously educate Rebekka for it. Vockerath's ideal

of free humanity is a hollow phrase. He ends his own life
not in order to save his soul from earthly entanglements,
but because he is a cowardly weakling unable to face his
duty. By their common death Rebekka and Rosmer atone
for their guilt and fulfill at the same time the ideal of a new
humanity for which Rosmer had fought. The beautiful
manner of their dying together is a sublime symbol of a
future possible advance toward an ever purer spirituality.
Vockerath's suicide is a pathological accident without any
interest. At the first performance in Berlin the entire
third act was omitted: no one missed it. C o l l e a g u e
C r a m p t o n (1892) is a lighter counter-part to T h e
P e a c e - F e s t i v a l. An artist, given to alcoholic excesses,
is on the point of ruin, when he is rescued by his brave
daughter and her lover. He has one more chance to reha-
bilitate himself as a citizen and an artist. While the play
ends with happiness and joy for all concerned, this too
seems only the postponement of an ultimate failure. Again
Hauptmann leads us into the environment of artists — he
had started out himself as a sculptor — with M i c h a e l
K r a m e r (1901), the fourth and last of the group designated as F a m i l y - p l a y s.

The painter Michael Kramer is a high-principled man,
an efficient artist, and one of those exceptional teachers
who know how to awaken in their pupils their very best
qualities and an enthusiasm for everything great and
sacred. Fate wills it that his own son alone resists his influence. Arnold, ugly and deformed, is also possessed of a
malicious character. His father has lavished upon him an

infinite measure of love and forbearance. In his pedagogic wisdom he sent Arnold to a distant city to study so that he might show what he could do, if left alone. The only result was another disappointment. Now, in a final conversation, the son is implored by his despairing father to unbosom himself, to tell the truth for once. Arnold lies, for his is a helplessly depraved soul. He remains stubborn and false.

For some time he has been imposing his attentions upon a bar-maid. To her he goes again. Teased and ridiculed by the girl's friends he draws a pistol, is quickly disarmed, and chased through the streets. Disgusted with his own wretchedness he drowns himself. — These are the events of three acts. In the fourth and last act we find Arnold's body in his father's studio.

What the complexities of life had frustrated again and again, has been accomplished by death. A hidden treasure has been unearthed. Father and son never could find the redeeming word which might have brought them together. Now at last Michael Kramer believes he understands his son. The dead child discloses to his parent a realm of beauty never before known, vistas into world-wide spaces and into the mysteries of the universe. The artist pays homage to his superior on the bier.

Death as the liberator and mediator: a lofty idea and capable of dramatic utilization; here unfortunately reached by a melodramatic sophism. The poet deceives his audience by making Michael Kramer deceive himself. In truth there was no treasure concealed in Arnold but an artistic talent.

This, it seems, surpassed his father's. Everything else that Michael Kramer claims to discover does not belong to the dead individual in particular but rather to the power of death as a natural phenomenon in general. The conclusion of this play too, then, is not so much an organic outgrowth of given premises as a disconnected addition: an epilog of illusion.

Indeed, we can imagine what the poet meant to say; only he failed to say it convincingly. The tragic idiosyncrasies and personal limitations of men of the same blood; the strange whim of Nature in granting the morally inferior one the greater talent; the decay of the latter; the solution of obscure riddles by death; the humble recognition of late insight: to make a drama out of such fertile motives Hauptmann did not possess enough of keenly consistent logic nor of combinative imagination.

In the mysticism of the end, as once before in a fragment H e l i o s (1896) he competes with Maeterlinck. But he lacked the delicate yet firm hand of the Belgian romanticist. In place of Maeterlinck's ethereal images with their fascinatingly transcendental symbolism Hauptmann gave wearisome speeches.

III.

Sudermann owed the enormous success of H o n o r and M a g d a to a shrewd compromise between the traditional society play and naturalistic technique. To a compromise between sentimental romanticism and stern natu-

ralism Hauptmann owed the popularity of H a n n e l e and
T h e S u n k e n B e l l (1893 and 1896). A young girl of
about twelve years lies dying in a village poorhouse the
inmates and milieu of which are depicted with pitiless
realism. Driven to despair by the brutality of her step-
father she tries to drown herself in a lake. Rescued from
the water she perishes in consequence of her exposure
and of long privation. In contrast to her hideous environment she has visions of her ascension to Heaven.

This is very pathetic and might even produce an effect
of grandeur, if, in the dream-parts, the author had not fallen
into a sentimental and bombastic mannerism of speech
doubly intolerable among the coarse bluntness of the
realistic parts. How gladly do we allow the ever glowing
yearnings of our youth to guide us back into the radiant
heavens of our childish fantasies! But Hauptmann's
Heaven is no abode for children or childlike grown people.
It is the invention of an affected estheticism. We are constantly reminded of Oscar Wilde's euphuism, when we read
phrases like this: "in thy palate grow may-lilies".

T h e S u n k e n B e l l is a symbol of F l o r i a n
G e y e r in which Hauptmann had in vain attempted a
drama of Shakespearian grandeur. "It sounds in the valley,
not on the heights". — The bellfounder Heinrich has
finished his best work. The new bell is destined for a
chapel high up in the mountains. But there the old pagan
forest-sprites are still holding their own against the advance
of the Christians from the valley. One of them hurls the
bell down into an abyss when it is about to reach the sum-

mit. And Heinrich follows his work. Mortally wounded he drags himself to the hut of a mysterious "bush-grand-mother", a personification of the primitive forces of nature. She waits upon Heinrich, assisted by the fair elf Rautendelein. Heinrich is found by his friends and carried to his home. Now the elf is seized by an irresistible longing for human love. For the first time in her life she weeps. Her soul is awakened. In spite of the warnings of the water-god Nickelmann who woos her, she goes down into the valley to Heinrich.

Disguised as a servant she enters his house, cures him through her witch-craft, and inspires him who had totally despaired of further work, to new creative will. He deserts his wife and children following Rautendelein into the mountains where he wishes to make a wondrous chime of bells for a Sun-temple. He feels himself master of the powers of nature, master of his art, master of men. He experiences the blissful ecstasy of the creative superman and disdains to heed the friendly warning of the priest who came up to him to remind him of his duties. And yet his haughty self-confidence is shaken. Besides, the sprites scorn him and sow doubt in his heart. In a dream he sees his children carrying a pitcher filled with their mother's tears. His wife has drowned herself in the mountan-lake where the bell had fallen. Her fingers touch the clapper. Sounds of woe and complaint reach up from the deep. Overcome with remorse Heinrich renounces Rautendelein to return to his fellow-men. But they now reject him. Homeless, friendless, ruined body and soul, despairing of his genius, he finds himself once more near the wood-hut. Once more Rautendelein, who has become Nickelmann's joyless bride, returns to him. In her last embrace he passes away. —

It has often been pointed out and need not be repeated here, how loosely the various motives from various sources are pieced together, how vague the characterization of persons, how painfully slow the action, how sentimental the language. That besides all deficiencies there are a stately number of truly beautiful passages goes without saying. In this connection only a few important things demand brief discussion.

First, T h e S u n k e n B e l l is a self-confession of the poet. His great work was a failure. The greater work which he then attempts with the assistance of superhuman powers is given up, after it has scarcely begun: it is beyond his strength. Like his Heinrich Hauptmann himself is a half-genius of the highest aspirations, at times revelling in the godlike ecstasy of unlimited faculties, yet repelled from his dreamed-of paradise again and again by his inner disunion. As his Heinrich became homeless so the poet wanders about between the extremes of a transcendental and materialistic view of life, between the extremes of an idealistic and realistic view of art, without taking root anywhere.

Second, his mental horizon is narrow even with regard to his inventions. He repeats himself and others (his sources) all too often. An essential part of the plot was taken over from L o n e l y P e o p l e. Heinrich is identical with Johannes Vockerath as the man between two women and as the "genius". The voluminous book which is never finished has changed places with the wonderful chime of the same fate. Heinrich like Johannes, and like Florian Geyer, is a hero only in theory. The poet takes recourse to proving his heroic qualities by conversational argumentation instead of making them a dynamic element in reality. — The inner discrepancies have their effect upon the form tearing wide crevices in the structure of the play.

*   *

*

Poor Henry (Der arme Heinrich 1902) is a modernized dramatization of Hartmann von Aue's little epic. The powerful count Heinrich is suddenly made an outcast by the most horrible of all diseases, leprosy, which he brought with him from a crusade. Despairing of life he retires into the loneliness of one of his rural estates where he is taken care of by his faithful tenant Gottfried. There is no help for him, for the only means of recovery he could never accept, even if it were offered to him: there is a physician at Salerno who cures leprosy through the heart-blood of a pure virgin voluntarily sacrificed.

The tenant's daughter hears of this. Ever since a child she has had an enthusiastic admiration for her lord; now at the threshold of womanhood, she is filled with impassioned sympathy the cause of which is an unconsciously developing sexual love. At the same time she is a devout Christian knowing of no higher ideal than heavenly beatitude. And there is, she reasons, no safer path to Heaven than her self-sacrifice. She offers her life to her lord.

But Heinrich, a noble character to the core, rejects her. He is incapable of an egotism that lives by the destruction of an innocent one. Impelled by her religious-sexual mania Ottegebe persists in forcing herself upon him. Heinrich's will-power grows in proportion to the increasing measure of temptation. He successfully battles against his craving for life so strangely incited. — These scenes of temptation and hard-won victory show Hauptmann's art at its best. Here he approaches occasionally grandeur, would indeed reach it, if he possessed the ability of sustaining his effects.

Heinrich shakes off Ottegebe. He seems definitely exposed to the indescribable misery of the leper, an object of horror to himself and mankind, annihilated for ever. — But misery is too great. Like a worm trampled upon he turns against his fate. The instinct of life re-awakens. He wants to live — to live at any price. In a trance-like state of passion he seeks and finds Ottegebe who is concealed in a hermitage. Now he accepts her offer; and she is willing as ever.

What follows next takes place between the fourth and fifth acts, corresponding exactly to Hartmann's story. They come to the Salerno physician. The girl is fastened to the operating-table. At the sight of this Heinrich gains control of himself once more. Definitely overcoming his egotism he prevents the sacrifice being made for him. And

— he is cured. Not by the blood of a fellow-creature but by the radical change of his innermost nature. God gives him back to himself, to the world, to happiness, in reward for his self-abnegation. And yet this miracle was after all brought about by Ottegebe's love; for it was her unselfishness that generated his.

Heinrich returns home with Ottegebe, a new man. He makes her his wife who at last discovers the secret of her own soul.

As in Michael Kramer the theme is the redeeming force of death, so here the redeeming force of love. The poet had the following problems before him: what are the psychological currents that lead a doomed man to despair, to accepting an unheard-of sacrifice, finally to renouncing his personal claims to life? — The inner struggles of the man are intermingled with and influenced by no less painful turmoils in the soul of a young woman who, because of love for the stricken man and because of a fervid longing for the martyr's crown, decides to sacrifice her own life. Seeing her sacrifice at first rejected, she despairs of attaining her ideal until she is ultimatly given the opportunity to prove the sincerity and power of her love. The counterplot rests upon this latter problem. In the background of both problems stands the mystic riddle: can the sacrifice of one human being influence not only the psychological but also the physical nature of another?

Hartmann von Aue tells the inner and outer events in his simple and straightforward manner. His story is intended for readers who naïvely believe in miracles;

readers who know that the hope of a martyr's crown and of an eternal life inspired thousands to suffer a quick if cruel death. Even modern readers, however strongly determined by rationalistic considerations we may be, are able to appreciate the enchanting grace of the medieval poem. We follow the author back into an age, when signs and wonders still occurred, when the miraculous cure of a disease which defies modern medicine, was not an impossibility. We believe,: for "once upon a time it happened". From this point of view we may esthetically enjoy a similar legend according to which St. Odilia cured a leper by her loving embrace.

Hauptmann's attitude is different. He means to cast the old material into a new form. He means to motivate artfully what his predecessor naively told as an established fact. He travels the same paths as the neo-romanticists of Hugo von Hofmannsthal's type (E l e c t r a). To be sure, he does not call his play "a drama" but "a German legend" classing it with H a n n e l e and T h e S u n k e n B e l l as a "fairy-drama". However, there is no trace of fairyland during four acts. On the contrary, we have before us a so-called strictly scientific method of motivation. The girl's death-defying readiness for self-sacrifice is not represented as a universal fact necessarily resulting from a given environment, but as an exceptional case to be accounted for by abnormal psycho-physiological, by pathological conditions. Ottegebe's ecstasy is due to an unusual degree of nervousness in connection with her developing puberty. Not only Heinrich is sick but also his saviour Ottegebe.

The devils are to be cast out by Beelzebub, as it were. We are, therefore, compelled to scrutinize a motivation which is intended for giving proofs. The result is that we doubt the possibility of a cure. The miracle, as everything pertaining to it, is no longer a plain fact, acceptable on faith, but a problem subject to the criticism of our intellect. Consequently the fairy-tale collapses as a fairy-tale, the drama as a drama. Having followed a psychological drama of considerable interest through the fourth act, we are no longer in the mental attitude to absorb a fifth act which purports to be a legend. So soon as the poet treats a modern audience to the solid food of scientifically controllable motivation, he renders it unfit for enjoying the etherial ambrosia of miracles.

The drama ends with the fourth act; and it ends as a tragedy. Ottegebe and Heinrich set out to experience a terrible illusion, whether Ottegebe dies or lives. But Hauptmann never saw clearly, never thought logically. He did not realize whither his poetic instinct had directed him, i. e. to a drama quite independent of the epic source. He clung to the subject-matter. In order to conform to tradition he made his plausible modern tragedy end as an implausible c o m é d i e l a r m o y a n t e by means of an old-fashioned d e u s e x m a c h i n a.

The supreme law of the drama is the strictest consistency of idea. Hebbel's J u d i t h ends as a tragedy. The conclusion necessarily changed, after the premises had been changed. But can we expect logical consistency of the works, if their author is divided within himself?

Hauptmann has discarded the old Christian religion without
finding satisfaction in modern philosophy. He who is generally classed as a naturalist, is and has always been a god-
seeking romanticist: but does not admit that. If he were a
consistent naturalist he could give us fine stories of life.
If he were a consistent romanticist he could accomplish for
prose-fiction what Mombert is doing for the lyric. The
hybrid of scepticism and faith breeds hybrids. P o o r
H e n r y is a one-winged creature unable to rise from the
ground. The next fairy-drama stopped short b e f o r e
t h e s u m m i t was reached:

A n d P i p p a d a n c e s.

The scenes of E l g a (1896) are an unsuccessful dramatization of Grillparzer's story D a s K l o s t e r b e i S e n-
d o m i r. The fragment H e l i o s of the same year is a
study after Maeterlinck's mystic plays. S c h l u c k a n d
J a u (1900) is a bombastic dilution of the prelude to Shakespeare's T h e T a m i n g o f t h e S h r e w. A n d P i p p a
d a n c e s reminds us of Browning's P i p p a P a s s e s.
While the first three works fail to come up to the standard
of their models, the last one excels Browning's bookish
construction in true vitality and warmth of feeling. The
passing Pippa by her songs arouses the conscience of the
city's four "happiest" people. The dancing Pippa means
to four men the embodiment of their ideals of beauty and
happiness.

The scene of the first act is a tavern in the Silesian
mountains near the Bohemian frontier. The guests are

lumber-jacks, mechanics, glass-blowers from a neighboring factory. It is a mid-winter night. Scanty lamp-light, mixed with the rays of the moon, struggles against the hazy atmosphere of the smokefilled room. Tavern-keeper and waitress at the bar. Cardplayers at one table, the owner of the glass-works, "the director", at another. He, a man of about fifty, has come on horseback in order to see Pippa, the daughter of the Italian glass-blower Tagliazoni, dance. Pippa appears at her father's command, after a considerable sum of money has been paid to him. She is a delicate, almost heavenly beautiful, young girl with a wealth of hair the color of which is Tizian's auburn. A wonderful contrast, this radiant angel in an environment of filth and vulgarity. Hannele's apotheosis in the poor-house is here repeated with greater art. A cripple plays the ocarina. Pippa dances — dances with the hideous, gigantic, bear-like Huhn, a "spectre from the old glass-works who can neither live nor die". The dance consists in Pippa's continually trying to escape Huhn whom she fears and detests, who never ceases to pursue her.

Meanwhile there enters a new character: Michel Hell-riegel, a young, slender, sickly looking tramp. Shivering with cold he asks for a night's lodging. He, too, being a glass-blower, is on his way to Bohemia where he hopes to learn something extraordinary. In quest of the unknown, the ever luring distant ideal, he discloses rather than conceals, as he means to, his poverty, his weakness, his fear, his desires, by an over-flow of droll, mysteriously allusive speeches. The Director and Huhn instinctively divine their rival in him. For his youth and spirituality naturally supplement Pippa's.

The dance is interrupted by intensely dramatic events. Tagliazoni is detected as a cheater. Knives are drawn. The Italian flees, is chased by the crowd, overtaken, and stabbed to death. Hellriegel is turned out by the superstitious waitress as having brought bad luck with him. So Huhn and Pippa are left alone for a moment. This is Huhn's opportunity for which he has long been watching. He seizes her and carries her to his lonely shanty.

In the second act the real imperceptibly changes into the symbolical. Huhn, after carefully laying Pippa on a bed of rags, starts a fire in the stove. Again the contrasts: the delicate, helpless girl — the uncanny giant; the cold, dark hut — light and heat only next the fire-place. When Pippa awakens and realizes her situation she is overcome with horror. But Huhn quiets her, declaring that neither he himself nor any one else shall ever do her harm. Only she must stay with him. He has saved her from the Director who would have made her the toy of his carnal desires. To Huhn she is the fulfillment of vague dreams, of an ardent, semiconscious yearning for light, beauty, spirituality.

In strangely crude words of the touching simplicity of primitive men he attempts to say that there will come about a radical change in the world: it seems as though the limitation of the animal soul in him were fighting a tenacious struggle for the liberty of human intellect, for the happiness of a fully conscious perception of creation. When

Pippa touches his arm, he trembles and his heart almost bursts. The same primeval creative force which in Pippa has reached the stage of perfect beauty, vibrates in him too. He, in his crudity gives the glass its unshaped body. Pippa is the spark of fire that moulds the body into beautiful form. He is the very beginning of an evolution which with Pippa has come to its goal. Pippa is bound to him in a similar way as Nietzsche's superman to the ugliest man. He desires her but can never win her because of his individual limitation: her who would not exist but for that elemental collective power which lives in him. Since he is still in a chaotic state, she, Nature's most perfect ideal, abhors him as a mountain-climber may shun looking back into the precipice he ascended.

Huhn vaguely divines, Hellriegel intuitively feels his harmony with Pippa. Guided by the unerring instinct of his aspiration, the latter finds the way to the hut. At his approach Huhn, mad with jealousy, rushes out to drive him away. While the giant, blinded by a snow-storm, seeks for his rival in vain, Hellriegel enters unsuspecting. A magic music sounds now that the two whom fate has destined for each other, are alone. Beauty and the spiritualized yearning for beauty form a pure concord, while animal-man is capable of only the wild outcry "Youmalaï" which seems to express hope of universal joy.

Hellriegel has spent his last money in the tavern buying the cripple's ocarina. He feels that "the little gold-haired fairy" would have to emanate from it and dance, if he played on it. Without having noticed her as yet in the dark he begins to play, and suddenly she stands before him. Beauty voluntarily joins the idealist who, freed from material nature, strives for ever-higher forms of existence. Beauty becomes his guide, having herself been enriched with a soul, through his love, like the legendary elf. Together they flee from the threatening giant; while the music, by a mighty crescendo, announces the rise of the wintersun.

The last two acts take place in a cottage on the ridge of the mountains. A strange old man, Wann, lives there with his dumb servant. Wann appears to be a naturalist. He possesses an intimate knowledge of minerals, plants, animals, and men. He discovers all-embracing connections in minute details, and with his telescope he overlooks infinite spaces. No one knows exactly who he is. Now he seems an ordinary hermit, now a wise man who possesses superhuman powers, having solved the world's great riddle; now he resembles the bush-grandmother in T h e S u n - k e n B e l l, now he acts as the world's Ruler personified. For the characters of the play, at any rate, he is Providence. He says of himself that he is "waiting for the new beginning of and entrance into another musical-cosmic fraternity". This reminds us of Huhn's hope for universal bliss or of the old dreams of the "harmony of the spheres".

The Director, having lost Pippa, has come to Wann in order to find relief for his passion. Before being told, Wann has known all and even prepared a cure. By his magnetism he has attracted Hellriegel and Pippa who, through a furious blizzard, are wandering toward the land of their ideal. Pippa rushes in implaring the men to help poor Hellriegel who has broken down exhausted. While they are assisting Hellriegel, Huhn sneaks in and conceals himself in a corner. The Director realizes that he is superfluous here, for Pippa has forgotten him as well as her father completely. She lives only for the future, keeping alive hope in her lover's soul. The man of materialistic pleasure does not take part in such idealism. He disappears for ever.

Nursed by Wann and Pippa, Hellriegel recovers and at once begins to display a somewhat boastful optimism. But Wann proves his superiority. He shows Pippa the graceful model of a Venetian gondula whereupon she dimly remembers having seen similar vehicles in the past. She "comes from fairy-land and is about to return there". The gondula is the ship of imagination. The goal of Pippa's and Hellriegel's journey is Venice, the d o r a d o of glass-blowers; is Italy at large, the land of light and beauty. Distances dwindle away. They are no longer on a mountain pass between Silesia and Bohemia but at the gates of Sunny-land itself. And a journey in body is needless. By means of the gondula and of his peculiar gift of fantasy Hellriegel even now may see all that he is longing for, if Pippa swells his sails with the magic breeze. Imagination is inspired by love and beauty.

Under Wann's direction Pippa, rubbing the edge of a crystal-glass, generates wonderful music which transports Hellriegel into a hypnotic trance. The splendours of his dreams are revealed to him. But the divined presence of his enemy calls him back into plain reality, when he is just

on the point of reaching the final stage of his happiness.
Now Pippa falls asleep and is brought to an adjoining
room. Hellriegel too retires, while Wann promises to
keep watch.

If only doors and windows are well secured, no enemy
will be able to enter. But in Wann himself there has arisen
a passionate love for Pippa. Is he God-Creator who loves
His own creature and desires to have a share in human
happiness? Is he no God at all, only wisdom for ever shut
out from transient joys? At any rate he resigns, leaving
Pippa to the young visionary.

Now Huhn comes out from his hiding-place and sur-
prises Wann. Was the latter unable to save beauty from
the pursuit of its extreme contrast? Does not Providence
possess the power to interrupt the natural connections it
once established, to protect spirit entirely from matter?
The giant's coming Wann was unable to hinder, but he can
stay his brutal force of destruction. Wrestling with him
he inflicts a mortal injury upon him: "This snowed-in
hut of God contains no food for beasts of prey."

If Pippa is cautious, there will be no more danger for
her. The lovers return, excited over the combat. Now that
they see the giant suffer, he seems like a brother to them
whose pains fill them with sympathy. Even of Wann
Huhn is now a part: the one is a "man" the other wishes
to become a "man". Huhn's howling is the painful cry
of maddening perception of God. For his defeat has made
the giant conscious of his own inferiority, and there is
only one remedy for his despair: death.

To call in Death, as Wann desires him to, Hellriegel
is not courageous enough, thereby causing the catastrophe.
Wann must go himself, leaving the trio alone, after he has
warned Pippa not to dance in his absence. As Wann did
before, so now Pippa lays her hand upon Huhn's throbbing
heart. In his delirium he tells how people came to the
glass-works in order to seek for some light in their distress;
how one solitary little spark arose from the ashes illumi-
nating the world by its fitful flame. It is Pippa's dance.
Once more the giant wants to dance with her. Urged by
Huhn, Pippa gives way to the feeling, as though she really
were only a spark floating alone through infinite space.
A mysterious power forces her on, and yet she is warned
by a voice from within. At last Hellriegel, with sympathetic humor, encourages her to fulfill the giant's last wish.
Huhn's heart-beat grows more and more heavy, moving
not only Pippa and Hellriegel, but the whole earth which
trembles with thunder. And Pippa dances. "With the
music of the ocarina, played by Michel, Pippa makes painfully measured, somewhat convulsive, motions of dancing.
By and by her dance becomes wilder and like that of a
bacchante. A rhythmical tremor shakes the body of old
Huhn . . . From the deep of the earth come subdued
sounds."

At this moment Wann returns with Saviour Death.
(We are reminded of L'Intruse.) Thereupon Huhn
with a hateful glance at Wann crushes in his hand a drink-
ing-glass which Hellriegel had given him. Pippa trembles,
is seized with torpor; and, calling her lover's name once

more, she sinks dead into Wann's arms. Now Huhn
triumphantly cries out his Yumalaï and dies. In spite of
Wann's care the crude force of nature, unable to possess
Beauty, draws her with it to destruction, proving thereby
its ultimate oneness.

Beauty's concrete presence was not allotted permanently to the idealist either. Ideals are gifts of especially
blessed hours. Once recognized, they must not be desecrat-
ed through the contact with every day life. Only in
dreams they appear as the guiding stars.

Michel does not realize Pippa's death. He has become
blind without knowing it, for he is full of inner visions. He
sees only a rosy future before him and, in the midst of a
wintery environment, a magnificent spring-landscape.
With the help of the everlasting light in his breast, he feels
sure of his way through the night. By Wann, who is married to shadows, he is married to Pippa's shadow. Cosmic
spirit, a universal abstraction, not a physical and individual
phenomenon is the ideal of the far-sighted sage as of the
blind dreamer. Pippa whose momentary phase of existence
only has come to an end, is again far ahead upon her own
journey, the uncouth giant again following her. Nature
destroys the individual phenomenon; it preserves the type.
The contrast between rude strength and refined beauty is
eternal; likewise the longing for beauty.

The blind dreamer in his imagination anticipates the
bliss of permanent success: for him "Pippa dances". Certain
of peace and joy to come he leaves, happily giggling. But
the ocarina he plays brings forth "a heartrendingly sad

tune". Does Pippa's soul long for rest, for lasting happiness? If the optimistic player himself does not hear the lament, the sage who remains behind alone hears it. With a painful tone of renunciation he says: "Farewell, farewell little gondola". He understands the tragedy of a never ending quest. He would like to preserve the individual phenomenon in its peculiar charm; perhaps he would prefer the optimist's easier fate. But he can do nothing, since he realizes the necessity of eternal metamorphosis, since he has no control over the law of growth and decay (which he established himself?). Death whom he called to rescue the lovers took not only Huhn with him but also Pippa. Is Wann the God of Schopenhauer's pessimism or the tragically modified superman of Nietzsche? Or is he both? It may be that Pippa is meant to correspond to Nietzsche's conception of dance as the triumphant expression of a superior affirmation of life, of an enfranchisement and artistic shaping of all vital forces of man.

This attempt at interpreting Hauptmann's most philosophical work may have failed in many points. It seems indeed neither possible nor, according to an utterance of the poet himself, even desirable to explain all details. Pippa surpasses Hauptmann's other fairy-plays just for this reason: its symbolism is really deeply suggestive and full of significant possibilities, as is the case with the best of our ancient fairy-tales; and yet there is the one principal motif — as the spark of light — unmistakably kept up throughout: the longing for joy and beauty.

To raise And Pippa dances to the plane of a

classic the last two acts would have to be of the same compactness as the first half, which is indeed perfect. However, in the third and fourth acts there is unfortunately so much hasty sketching, so much lack of proportion that the desired emotional effect is not fully attained. In spite of this criticism it must be admitted that Hauptmann here succeeded in putting into concrete form what remained chaotic in his earlier plays of this type. A n d P i p p a d a n c e s is an almost worthy counterpart to the realistic W e a v e r s. We may, from a personal point of view, condemn the quest for the blue flower as a sterile mysticism. We cannot deny the fact that there is no poet living who, through the medium of the drama, found a more soul-stirring expression for that ever indelible craving of the human heart.

This relative height the poet has not reached again since. Here and there, e. g. H a n n e l e, M i c h a e l K r a m e r, had been noticeable a tendency toward bombastic phrases, hollow rhetoric, artificial perfume, studied pose. Such modern euphuism is in part responsible for the failure of C h a r l e m a g n e ' s H o s t a g e (K a i s e r K a r l' s G e i s e l 1908) and G r i s e l d a (1909).

IV.

E l g a was, as we have seen, a version of a story by Grillparzer. C h a r l e m a g n e ' s H o s t a g e is an imitation of Grillparzer's drama T h e J e w e s s o f T o l e d o. Young king Alfonso, who loves his queen more from duty than from inclination, meets in the Jewess Rahel, for the first time, woman's sensuous charms. Her love makes him neglect his obligations as a ruler. His country is threatened by an invasion of the Moors. The most loyal among his retinue, inspired by the queen, revolt, kill Rahel in order to do away with the evil's cause, and then surrender to the king's authority. Instead of punishing them Alfonso admits his own guilt and leads the faithful rebels against the national enemy: the guilt of each individual is to be atoned for by the devotion of all to the common good.

The essential features of this plot are repeated by Hauptmann. Both poets symbolize woman's demonic influence — Grillparzer by a portrait, Hauptmann by a ring. The latter, however, adds another problem. While Alfonso is young, Karl is a man of about sixty. The sub-theme consequently seems to be the late passion of a man of declining age for a young woman. Gersuind-Rahel is killed before Karl wins her. But his amorous desire has the same effect upon him as possession upon Alfonso. The Jewess Rahel and the Saxon hostage Gersuind resemble each other like sisters. Both belong to a despised people so that their power is ascribed to witchcraft. Both are characters of primitive animal instincts, endowed with those magnetic sexual charms that explain the passion of men for them — to a certain degree.

Rahel's charm vanishes with her life. Alfonso never having known voluptuousness before, Rahel's immense fascination for him was as natural as his sudden disenchantment upon seeing her dead. She looks malicious to him.

His passion had been satisfied once for all. And besides, he had always entertained compunctions in the midst of his enjoyments.

Karl idealizes Gersuind, because she never was his, and because old age never ceases to long for the vigor of youth. But this psychologically fine motif is disturbed and made ineffective by foreign elements. First: Gersuind means only one of many love-adventures of an absolute ruler bound by no convention. Second: Gersuind's sensuality is exaggerated to such a degree of perverse bestiality as to exclude her from the sphere where human sympathy is possible. Still less than after Arnold Kramer's mean conduct, can we here believe in the feelings which her death is supposed to arouse in Karl. Although he knows that Gersuind committed acts of indescribable shamelessness, he is made to say: "Pain was her fate, pride and pain". With Grillparzer death reveals the true character; with Hauptmann death creates an impossible deception.

Yet this is not the only fault. The contrast between old age and youth, tragic in itself, is not made a propelling factor in the drama. Kars assures us at Gersuind's bier that nothing is left of him for his people but an old man, that his youth has faded away with the girl. But this we can at best take as an accidental fact; it is not the effect of causal connections. For on the one hand Karl is represented to be as vigorous, physically and mentally, as any young man; on the other hand his years did not, from Gersuind's point of view, form an obstacle at all. She ultimately loved him. She would, at their very first meeting, have given herself to him even without love, as she did with any man, if he only took her. He refrained from making her his mistress for reasons quite outside any consideration of his age.

In brief, the various elements, dramatic or tragic, were not welded together into a unit, nor was any single one clearly worked out. There is again an amazing want of logical consistency. And, as in previous plays, there is more talking than doing. Grillparzer was not entirely free from this tendency in his J e w e s s o f T o l e d o. But he was conscious enough of the requirements of his form to make even long speeches serve some dramatic purpose. And he knew how to condense, in a critical moment, the situation into one word. When Alfonso, still quivering with wrath, thunders his "guilty" against the rebels, their leader, Manrique, replies: "And thou art not?" A word whose terrible pregnancy achieves a most powerful effect, bringing the king to his senses. Hauptmann, in his corresponding scene, uses more than a page of verses. C h a r - l e m a g n e ' s H o s t a g e is a typical work of weakly imitation.

G r i s e l d a stands even lower in the scale. It is the most contradictory, unnatural, bombastic of all of Hauptmann's productions. Boccaccio's well-known story is here dramatized in "ten scenes" or tableaux. The count's cruel treatment of his innocent wife is explained by his jealousy of their own child: an orgy of beastly sadism, finished by a compromise of melodramatic sentimentality. Equally unworthy of the author is his last play T h e R a t s (1911) where the longing of a childless woman for an offspring grows to criminal mania. In both works there is a poetical, even dramatic, germ buried in a chaos of intellectual and artistic aberrations.

V.

Hauptmann's literary career presents the bewildering phenomenon of an author who tenaciously clings to a form of expression quite contrary to the natural tendency of his genius. As if by chance he strikes, once or twice, a dramatically fruitful vein. The vast majority of his "dramatic" production is as undramatic as imaginable, whatever point of view we may take. He does not, in his tragic plays, make men of active energy, positive volitions, the centers of his plots. His heroes are sufferers resisting more or less strongly an impending doom the cause of which lies beyond the sphere of their wills. They lack the impulsive force of initiative. They never fight against powers of proportionate weight; nor does their fate — martyrs if they must be — ever reach the overwhelming grandeur of characters like Oedipus or Polyctetes.

In the comical genre Hauptmann created Frau Wolff but without opposing to her an adequate counterforce. The Beaver-Cape, as well as The Red Cock or Colleague Crampton, are mere successions of humorous scenes, no comedies.

Wherever dramatic possibilities seem to be devised, they are not turned to account. The conclusions are generally voluntary additions rather than catastrophes necessarily resulting from the original idea. Realizing this conspicuous discrepancy between dramatic form and undramatic content, Hauptmann endeavored to justify his method theoretically. In the preface to the collection of his works he says: "All thinking is based upon intuition. Thinking is also a struggle: consequently dramatic. Every philosopher who presents to us the system of his logic constructions, erected it from decisions reached through the party-strives of the voices of his soul: accordingly I consider the drama the expression of an original process of thinking, upon a high stage of development, without, to be sure, reaching those decisions which the philosopher is concerned about. From this view-point result inferences which infinitely extend the sphere of the drama in all directions beyond the conventional canons so that nothing perceived by our outer or inner senses can be excluded from this form of thinking which has become a form of art."

It is superfluous to point out the sophistic disregard of the essential problem, the romantic confusion, underlying this argumentation. Hauptmann's deductions, far from touching upon the drama as such, might be applied to the lyric and epic, in fact to any expression and communication through words, music, color, gesture, of what not. In the last analysis any effort of the brain, any manifestation of life is a "struggle". The question at issue is whether or not there is a conflict of wills and whether or not the final catastrophe is the necessary effect of given causes. The catastrophe of K i n g L e a r does not, indeed, bring about a decision, philosophical or unphilosophical. The world, at the close of the fifth act, looks no less contradictory than at the opening of the first. But the conflict between Lear's senile idiosyncracy and his brutal environment is depicted as a necessary and mighty battle of principles and brought to the catastrophe foreshadowed by the premises. Lear even in his madness is a king. Hauptmann writes tragedies of "geniuses" who are mediocrities. There is the rub. "Thinking", indeed! Only Hauptmann is not favored with that intellectual superiority which comprises a world, to reproduce it as a microcosm. His mental horizon is narrow. He is the poet of social sympathy in a limited sense. The aspirations, longings, sufferings of the lowly in spirit and rank are his domain. Great minds, types of advanced culture, revolutionizing events are beyond his grasp. Viewed from within his peculiar province he is a master whom we love and respect. Viewed as a world-poet he is exasperatingly disappointing. He starts from combinations of keenly observed details, seeks for wide connections, reaching these here and there, but never able to hold his threads in a firm hand. Even a chaos is subject to artistic organization, if it is to make the effect of chaos rather than of unintentional confusion.

Hauptmann's first work was a verse-epic modelled after Byron's C h i l d e H a r o l d (P r o m e t h i d e n - L o s 1885). This was withdrawn from the market by its author. In 1887 and 1890 respectively appeared the short stories R a i l w a y - G u a r d T h i e l and T h e A p o s t l e. Both testifying to a considerable talent for narration, some

critics have urged Hauptmann to try for the laurels of an
epicist. He would probably succeed in writing short stories
or "Novellen". His recent attempt at a prose-epic of greater
dimensions was an artistic failure. The epic requires as
high a degree of organizing power as the drama.

The Apostle is a modern Rousseauite. He despi-
ses civilization, making it responsible for all the misery of
the world. If only mankind returned to nature, to a simple
mode of living, there would be universal peace, paradise
on earth. This peace he sets out to preach. He fancies
himself in the rôle of a Messiah, pendulating between
studied pose and natural conviction. He is naïveté and
selfconceit combined. Traveling on foot he comes to a
large city. Here, ridiculed by the inhabitants for his
phantastic costume, his high-strung feelings temporarily
yield to sober meditation. But his illusion returns, when
crowds of children wonderingly follow his every step. The
resolution to preach his message to the nations awakes with
new force. Leaning against the railing of a bridge, he has
a vision of his triumphant announcement of world-peace.
Then he dreams that Christ dissolves his body and soul in
him. He becomes a religious maniac hearing himself commune with God as the Son of God.

This fine psychological study is the nucleus of a novel,
published twenty years later, The Fool in Christ
Emmanuel Quint. We have seen how deeply Haupt-
mann was concerned with the problem of redemption.
Hannele, Michael Kramer, Poor Henry,
Pippa are filled with a mystic longing for redemption

9*

from earthly limitations. In his early years Hauptmann experienced pietistic influences and never in his life again he entirely freed himself from the romantic mysticism of the Moravian Brothers. A pupil of ultradarwinian Haeckel, he attempted to make Christ his own on the basis of modern philosophy. There is a trustwortly report that he wrote a L i f e o f J e s u s which he did not publish. The Vionese theologian Karl Beth is probably right in supposing that this L i f e o f J e s u s was incorporated in the novel. Nearly all important events in the life of Jesus have their parallels in E m m a n u e l Q u i n t. The hero grows up in the house of a carpenter who is not his father. He is baptized in a brook, a dove soaring over him. He gathers disciples about him one of whom is a Judas. He meets Marys and Marthas and Magdalenes. He purifies a temple, performs miracles, calls the children to him, preaches, associates with sinners, comes in conflict with the scribes and with the government, is innocently arraigned, cast into prison, despised. Here the parallel ends. Emmanuel Quint is acquitted. The crime he had been accused of was committed by his Judas who hanged himself at the place of his deed. Forsaken by all his friends Emmanuel wanders about, nowhere finding a shelter; for his constantly repeated answer to all inquiries is: "I am Christ." Finally two herdsmen in the Alps take pity on him. Attempting to reach Italy (like Hellriegel), he freezes to death on a mountain-pass.

This story is built up in three layers. First comes what seems to be the L i f e o f J e s u s referred to: an attempt similar to those of D. F. Strauss and Renan only adapted to a modern environment according to the method of Fritz von Uhde's paintings. The problem would, then, be like this: what would mankind's attitude be to-day, if Christ appeared for the first time? What would be the character of Christ himself?

The second layer of the story begins with Emmanuel's communion with Christ. The scene of The Apostle is repeated and enlarged upon in the way of medieval mysticism. Emmanuel, in prison, has a vision which for him assumes the importance of a most powerful actual experience. "Quint and the Saviour's figure, like loving brothers who long have missed each other, meeting with outstretched arms, quite literally stepped into each other so that Quint felt the Saviours body and entire being enter him and dissolve in him. This experience was at the same time so incredible and wonderful because of its perfect reality," etc.

We face the problem of re-incarnation: how would the world receive Christ, if he came once more? This question is clearly raised by the author without any irony, scepticism, or supposition of pathological illusions; quite in contrast to The Apostle, where from the beginning we have a story of mental derangement before us. However, the third layer crowds out the two preceding problems.

Much to our amazement we observe how the poet forces himself to transform his Saviour and his modernized Franciscus into a maniac. Now we understand the reason why, during the first part, the hero sometimes is called a

fool, although he never acts as a fool: it is a mere re-
touching devise. The sublime subject grew beyond Hauptmann's creative faculties. His soul's insatiable craving had,
out of every day surroundings, built up the consoling apparition of The Saviour. It was not — we follow Karl Beth's
enlightening analysis — the d i v i n e Saviour, not the
heroic genius whose power conquered the world, but the
humble friend of the poor and oppressed, the personification of absolutely unselfish love. Onesided as the author's
view-point was: he had indeed created a character of such
fascinating sweetness, purity, goodness, as to win our
hearts completely. But, doubting the work of his own
hands, he despairs of having made his readers believe in it.
Seduced by rationalistic scepticism, he destroys his mystic
creation. Again the temple he had meant to build changed
into a hopeless labyrinth of negation.

V.

Arno Holz

———

A history of the determining influence of material conditions upon art has not yet been written. Modern German literature furnishes an important chapter. Gerhart Hauptmann, blessed with financial prosperity from his youth on, supported by a mighty clique of critics, the absolute master of his time, develops his talent to its limits. When forced by domestic troubles to meet extraordinary financial obligations, he becomes hasty, appeals frequently to the taste of the masses; his works no longer reach the stage of maturity. And his eulogists face the ungrateful task of explaining a conspicuously long series of failures. This fact raises the question, if Hauptmann ever could have succeeded under less favorable circumstances. — Arno Holz, his teacher, has always been persecuted by misfortune. He at no time was socially or economically independent. Rarely he was granted temporary moments of leisure. Whatever he achieved was wrested from the oppressing tyranny of poverty. He owes nothing to others, everything to his invincible energy, to a heroic idealism which links him with the few men of Schiller's type. If the coterie of critics that raised Hauptmann on the shield had had their own way entirely, Holz's life-work would have been totally ignored. He never had more than a few friends who understood him, and the official historians of literature do not yet do him justice, although he approaches his fiftieth year.

Arno Holz was born in 1863 in the province of East-Prussia, came to Berlin as a boy, published a few volumes of poetry at the age of twenty, and made himself first known as a contributor to M o d e r n e   D i c h t e r - c h a r a k t e r e (1885), an anthology of lyrics by the "Youngest Germans". His fiery and well-composed verses surpassed by far the average of the book. When, in the same year, another collection of his own poetry appeared: T h e B o o k   o f   T h e   T i m e   (B u c h   d e r   Z e i t,   L i e d e r e i n e s   M o d e r n e n), he was hailed by competent critics as the greatest lyrical genius of his generation and even awarded a prize by the Augsburg Schiller-Foundation. Not only was the versification strictly perfect — in more than four hundred pages there could be found not a single impure rhyme, and the strophic structure vied with Platen and Geibel in smoothness and sonority — but the contents were largely new. Holz attacked the existing order of things in life and literature as effectively as Heine had done. It was the revolutionary spirit that gave the book its weight. As youthfully romantic an idealist as there ever was, Holz had a keen eye for the esthetic values of present reality. He did not neglect the mysterious rustling in the forests, nor the soothing breezes of spring-nights and the suggestive ruins of ancient castles as poetical subjects. No one ever treated such conventional themes as these with greater skill nor with more typically German sentimentality. But also in the coal-dust and smoke of mines and factories, in the hammering of machines, in the roar of rail-ways, he heard soul-stirring music and saw the Nibelung's gold of poetry glitter.

With the touchingly grotesque extravagance of youth he joins the ranks of the modernists, battling against tradition in art and public life. As a poet of revolt he was characterized by Laurie Magnus in T h e F o r t n i g h t l y R e v i e w of 1897. The English critic is right in making the poet's years and the contemptible byzantinism of his fellow-countrymen responsible for the embittered hatred of church and state which flames up every-where, sometimes (as with Heine) approaching the blasphemous. Nevertheless Arno Holz, like Catullus, Shelley, Burns, is not excluded from immortality: "may not Germany one day raise to Arno Holz his marble tribute of a dome?"

There was a constructive side to Holz's lyrical rebellion, pointing to the future. He succeds in bringing home to his readers the grandeur of the new era with its gigantic struggle for truth and liberty, for a new social order. He makes us believe with him that there is coming something greater and mightier than the past, that the day is dawning the first lark of which he wishes to be, the day of truth, liberty, honor, love — love for all men, for all nations. He too shouts his "Be embraced, ye millions", no less rich in universal sympathy, no less enthusiastically striving for the eternal good, no less hopeful than Schiller just a century before him.

An important achievement had thus been attained: a wide extension of the field of lyrics which in itself meant a victory over the sweetish poets of the day as indisputable as that won by Liliencron's A d j u t a n t e n r i t t e. And yet, the artist in Holz was dissatisfied. He, "the greatest form-talent" among the "Youngest Germans" recognized that his victory was only a temporary one, if the new contents did not find a new form. A new and adequate technique, however, was impossible so long as the relation of the artist to his source of inspiration, i. e. the relation of art and nature, was entangled in the wilderness of such contradictory theories and methods as were current at that time.

Speculative esthetics, in Germany as elsewhere had, under Kant's influence, drifted farther and farther away from the life-center of art. It was concerned about an a-priori-ideal of beauty instead of the problem of expression, about the psychology of the non-artist instead of the psychology of the artist. From this onesided standpoint esthetics assumed the task of forcing all art into the strait-jacket of abstract systems. It was not until Taine came to prominence that science once more taught men to appreciate art as a natural phenomenon in connection with general evolution. Taine's theory of the "m i l i e u" was in effect a revelation, although it was but a repetition and late justification of Herder's ideas who, in his struggle against Kant's transcendental esthetics for an empirical science of art, had met with a humiliating, if temporary, defeat.

However, Taine was as little consistent as Schiller and Goethe. These great poets, in their esthetic theories,

vacillated between the experiences of their creative instincts and the spell of Winckelmann's and Kant's academic
speculations. Speaking as artists, they declared art a
natural phenomenon and the individual work of art to be
tending toward the effect of a work of nature. Speaking as
the pupils of Winckelmann and Kant, they claimed for art
the place of a metaphysical miracle above nature. Likewise
Taine declares that every work of art is the result of a
given m i l i e u. On the other hand he asserts that art
does not consist in reproducing effects of nature. The
former statement, Holz recognizes, is a new empirical
law; the latter an old unproven dogma.

The confusion of this theory is outdone by Zola. Art
being a phenomenon subject to certain laws, he mistakes
the analytical method of science for the formative synthesis
of art. He strives for truth and yet he allows the individual's temperament as much arbitrariness as ever was
allowed by speculative idealism. Art in general is for him
the result of natural laws: a work of art in particular the
result of individual independence.

Such confusion was impossible with a man who, in a
singular degree, combined the creative faculty of the artist
with the analytical intellect of the thinker. If the artist is
an infinitesimal part of the universe, it necessarily follows
that nature's means are at his disposal in a relative proportion. Besides, his technical means of expression are largely symbolical. Neither any single work of art, then, nor
art in general can ever attain the total effect of nature.
On the other hand it is evident that it has always been

the aim of art to reproduce (express) impressions of nature. And this, indeed, is all that can be said of the law-
ful function of art. So we have the formula: "art has the
tendency to be nature again; it becomes nature in proportion to its means and their application."

This art-law, expounded in a booklet D i e K u n s t
(1891), was both too true and too simple to be understood
by scholasticism. Except for his fellow-artists to whom
Arno Holz merely gave an old truth in a surprisingly concise form, critics joined in a hysterical condemnation of
what they considered an anarchistic plot against the sanctuary of esthetic tradition. The very word "nature" was
misunderstood. The non-artists — and any critic as such
is a non-artist — identified their own limited power of
reception with the infinitely greater one of the artist.
They mistook "nature" for external matter, instead of
recognizing the fact that everything that happens within
the wide expanse of outer nature as well as within man's
soul is "nature". Every idea, every perception, every
sentiment is nature. The artist being a part of nature
himself, not only his esthetic experience but also its reflex
in art would have to be called "nature". In this sense
Herder and Goethe really declared works of art to be
works of nature, and there would be a veritable c i r c u -
l u s v i t i o s u s of conceptions of "nature". But Arno
Holz, like his predecessors, knows that general nature
creates from an infinite abundance, the individual artist
from most narrow limitations. So he assumes the following gradation: primary nature, i. e. the cause of esthetic

experience; secondary nature, i. e. the esthetic experience itself, respectively its inner form; tertiary nature, i. e. the latter's reflex in the visible work of art. This tertiary nature (= art, work of art) may, then, be compared to the shadow which a sun-lit tree casts upon the earth. For the artist the outer form of his vision is no more than a shadow, a colorless outline of the real picture. For the non-artist, to be sure, even this outline will be a revelation, will call forth emotions of which he either was incapable, at the sight of primary nature, or for which he found no expression.

Such incapability makes the non-artist say: "art surpasses nature and this superiority is its chief virtue". And the same mental defect, supported by certain crass eccentricities of would-be artists, makes scholastic criticism condemn naturalism, as if it ever had demanded a mechanical reproduction, a photography, a phonographic copy, not of the essence of nature, but of its most superficial aspects. So even Taine, from a comparison of a Grecian marble-statue with a medieval saint's image, concluded that the aim of art could not possibly be an exact reproduction of nature. For, he says, in the latter nature is obviously imitated to an extreme limit: real garments, genuine jewelry etc., while in the former with its uniform tinting, with its eyes lacking their balls, that limit is not approached by far. — On the contrary, Holz replies to this inference, the Greek statue approaches nature much more nearly than does the saint's image. The Greek worked according to the laws of his material. To the pious image-carver it never occurred that he departed from nature to the same degree as he violated the conditions peculiar to his material. The Greek was an artist, the Catholic image-carver an artisan.

"Art has the tendency to be nature again." It is the artist's instinctive aim to create a work which, as an organism perfect in itself, corresponds to his vision of primary nature. In order to attain his end he uses the technical means of his individual art, the possibilities of his personal faculty, of his social and political environment, of his native soil, of the boundlessly manifold conditions of life in general: "Nature, Nature, and Nature again! There is no salvation outside of her, and our most sublime achievements are only faint reflections of her billion times billion multiplicities." Consequently it is the task of the science of art to investigate and explain the respective relation of works of art to nature, of the real attainment to the ideal aim. Since every single work is an organism, art in general a cosmos of organisms, it cannot be the task of science to prescribe the artist's course, just as botany cannot precribe the growth of plants. The science of art must restrict itself to the interpretation of art-phenomena and become a part of psychology which as such is concerned about the psyche of both artist and non-artist.

The art-law does not state a dogma but a fact. It is not a definition of "what is art"? but presupposes the existence of art, negating all that does not tend toward nature. In this way the knowledge of the law exercises a clarifying and stimulating influence upon the young artist.

It tells him that he is a link in a progressive chain of evolution, that he is not superior to nature but a dependent part of nature. It tells him that art is not a voluntary play but a necessary expression of life. It tells him that he must create according to the conditions of his own self, that he must grasp nature and attempt to form his impressions of her not like Sophocles or Phidias or Shakespeare or Rembrandt or Goethe before him, not looking backwards but with his eye on present and future. The law tells him that art does not follow an a-priori-canon of beauty but that each work of art is the nearer perfection the more closely it approaches the unity of material and form, the goal: nature, where body and soul are one.

The ossified dogma of beauty, as borrowed from a foreign, only half-understood, civilization, is replaced by the evolutionary principle of unity of style. The form always results from the subject's innermost nature. The Ego's arbitrariness disappears and things speak their own language. The conditions of a work of art once given, they will not be disturbed. The phantasies of aërial dreams, left to themselves, are nature no less than is earthly concreteness. The ideal of truth merges into the ideal of beauty. Schiller's conception of the self-determination of art is realized. The German artist, at last, becomes conscious of h i s nature. With means of his own he expresses a world of his own. He no longer disguises his national subjects in foreign masks. He proudly feels his art grow with the deepening of his racial instincts.

Born from an evolutionary spirit, the law excludes

any kind of scholasticism. "All previous theories considered art an a b s o l u t u m. This law, based upon a
different view of life, says it is a r e l a t i v u m. It says:
there is no art p e r s e for us human beings, as there is no
nature p e r s e. There exist just as many conceptions of
art as there exist corresponding conceptions of nature.
No two conceptions can possibly be alike. The same
work of art, if viewed by two different people, is no longer
the same. Nay, it is not even the same, if viewed by one
individual at two different times. This necessarily causes
the immense diversity of our judgments."

The art-law, furthermore, is progressive. It does not
assert that there are so and so many arts: music, painting,
sculpture, poetry etc. but,: there are as many arts as there
are means of expression. Their effects being gradually
exhausted, they are replaced by new means or by new
combinations of old ones.

The art-law also makes possible a statics as well as a
dynamics of the arts. That art which conforms to the law
most closely is superior in value to the rest. Since there
is no means of expression more universal than language,
poetry is first in order.

Lastly the art-law shows how the development of
every art depends primarily upon the development of its
means, and how this development continually tends toward
one and the same goal: nature. The absurdity of norma-
tive esthetics is thus definitely proven in spite of the lamen-
tations of academic non-artists, however scholarly they
may be.

The art-law, once fully understood, will form the basis
of a real science of art, for it enables us to appreciate art
in its widest aspects as a medium of expression, as nature's
unceasing endeavor of self-revelation. Arno Holz, out-
lining the plan of this science, unconsciously unearthed the
treasure which Herder had gathered, which Goethe and
Schiller did not sufficiently value.

II.

New means of expression for the spirit of a new time!
In pictorial art the problem had been solved. The masters
of Barbizon, as early as in the second quarter of the 19th
century, had accomplished the fundamental work. Men
like Uhde, Leibl, Zügel, Kalckreuth, Liebermann, without
endangering their national and personal character, were
able to adopt and develop the French technique. They
were the peers of their more renowned French contemporaries.

In literature conditions were different. Complexes
of colours, light, and air, and the rhythm of contours cause
direct sensations, being, to a certain degree, objective
means of expression: they, like music, speak an international language.

The attempt to import Zola's naturalism into Germany
in the same way as pleinairism was a failure. Chiefly for
two reasons: first, Zola was entirely formless. His anxious
respect for external facts ("human documents"), his pe-
dantic determinism, chained him so tightly to the detail,

10*

to the environment in a narrow sense, as to break up the perspectivity of his composition. Zola, as an artist too, vacillated between the old and the new. A conqueror of new material, he by no means surpassed the art of the best German contemporaries of the old school: Keller and Storm.

Second: the German Zolaists like Kretzer and Conrad did not stop to think that poetry, in contrast to figurative art, depends upon indirect effects. Language merely suggests ideas, emotions, visions; it is not a reality in itself. It is symbolical, as Herder had recognized when he wrote his supplement to L a o c o o n. It was, therefore, impossible to learn from the literary technique of the French in the same direct manner as from their pictorial art. — Out of the very spirit of the German language there had to be created a word-technique rivalling the increased facilities of the other arts.

F l a u b e r t in his M a d a m e B o v a r y (his other works remained comparatively unknown in Germany) had furnished a model of naturalistic style. Here there was a human life visualized with a variety of characteristic details, with a unity of composition, with a matter-of-fact objectivity, steadiness, and firmness which were the result of an infinitely painstaking and laborious devotion to and self-sacrificing identification with the essence of the material. Here language was applied with a strict consideration of word-values, with an insight into respective shades of meaning, with a control over the total effect, in brief, with a purity of style unparalleled in the history of prose-fiction.

Here, at last, the artist completely gave way to his creation, checking the fire of personal passions in himself in order to t r a n s m i t it with all the greater heat to his characters as their individual source of life.

Such a word-technique had to be found for Germany, if the superficial and imitative mediocrities, the conventional trash which the gentle readers indulged in, were to be permanently cleared away. Arno Holz accomplished this task.

His was a nature like Flaubert's: a volcanic temperament within, an iron power of self-control in his relation to his esthetic experiences. He did not imitate Flaubert but he learned from him whatever there was to be learned. He experimented as long, as untiringly and honestly redressing his errors, as wholly devoted to mother nature as were Rousseau, Corot, and Diaz, Manet and Monet, and Flaubert. His first productions in the new technique seemed insignificant. There were a few prosesketches and a tragic Christmas play: every day subjects, impressions of the life of common people; mostly written in co-operation with Johannes Schlaf. The sketches appeared first under the misleading title P a p a H a m l e t by "Bjarne Holmsen" and were subsequently re-published with the play (F a - m i l i e S e l i c k e) as N e w P a t h s (N e u e G l e i s e) in 1889.

However, these studies, without being imitations, possessed style in Flaubert's strict sense; and they were characteristically German. Here once more real human beings were speaking a natural language, were living and moving about by themselves. They were no mechanical puppets nor silhouettes pasted on a flat background. They appeared in the brilliant variety of colors, in the everchanging illuminations of their environments. So there was opened an inexhaustible source of esthetic values, the existence of which no one else had even dreamed of before.

If to this intensely radiant, warm, and differentiating characterization came consistency of composition and greatness of subject, there was established a new kind of novel and drama as different from Goethe's novel and Schiller's drama as they from Cervantes and Shakespeare.

In this respect, for the drama, Ibsen had done the necessary work of preparation: by the penetrating truth of his psychology, by the logical consistency and compactness of his motivation, by the clear transparency of his structure. Ibsen, toward the end of the eighties, having overcome the impassioned resistance of conventional criticism, was more and more recognized as the leading master of the drama in Europe. In Germany, where his works, partly under his personal supervision, were given model performances, he was perfectly at home. Theaters, critics, and aspiring playwrights gradually disregarded his being a foreigner. The German drama, for a considerable time resting upon his shoulders, took as onesided a course of development as the novel of the Zola-disciples. It was not until many years after the beginning of the modern movement that the German drama was finally enfranchised, when Arno Holz succeeded in finding the synthesis of his impressionistic word-technique and Ibsen's dramatic

method; i. e. with his tragedy B e a t r i c e (S o n n e n-
f i n s t e r n i s), 1908.

For what he had done in 1889 he received no reward
other than the consciousness of his own value. Honor and
fame fell to the share of his most talented pupil, Gerhart
Hauptmann, who dedicated his first play to "Bjarne Holmsen, the most consistent realist, for his decisive encourage-
ment". The master himself, persued by life's meanest
calamity, poverty, was lost to literature for years. When,
in 1896, he published S o c i a l A r i s t o c r a t s, one of
Germany's finest comedies, he was ignored or misunderstood. And again, twelve years afterwards, when B e a-
t r i c e appeared, he had to undergo the same disheartening
experience.

The subject of B e a t r i c e is similar in terribleness
to Sophocles' O e d i p u s, to Hartmann's G r e g o r i u s,
to Shelley's T h e C e n c i (Holz's heroine calls herself
Beatrice Cenci), to Ibsen's R o s m e r s h o l m. Its treatment is unassailably chaste; the ethical principle underlying
as stern as in T h e B r i d e o f M e s s i n a and T h e
S c a r l e t L e t t e r.

The painter Hollrieder devotes his entire energy to
his art without attaining to that degree of perfection which
he rigidly demands of himself. Isolated from the world,
despairing of his art, he has reached a stage of hopeless
pessimism. Only one friend is left to him, Url who shares
his apartments. Through Url he meets a beautiful actress
"Beatrice". She is the first woman to make an impression
upon him, except for a young girl whom, many years be-

fore, he rescued from the water, and who never was heard of again. Love of life and confidence in his art arise in him once more. Beatrice, at his request, poses for part of a picture. Under her inspiration the new work becomes Hollrieder's grandest achievement. To his mute wooing, however, Beatrice does not respond, although she loves him. She has recognized in him her rescuer and considers herself unworthy of him. For there is a terrible guilt weighing upon her soul. The secret of this guilt, Beatrice's past, is gradually disclosed, chiefly through the malicious efforts of Hollrieder's former pupil and associate Musmann who, mentally deranged, is obsessed with a diabolical hatred and jealousy of the man, his superior in character and in artistic talent. "Beatrice" is the daughter Sibylla of Hollrieder's former teacher Lipsius. Her father's crime, her own partial guilt she attempted to atone for by voluntary death. — Hollrieder, after learning the truth, at first seems to overcome his horror. Love, art, life, win a temporary victory which is turned to a catastrophe by Hollrieder's sensitiveness. The drama, then, represents the struggle against the power of the past for happiness in the present and future.

B e a t r i c e grew out of the poet's most personal experiences. Hollrieder is largely Arno Holz himself: the artist who, striving for the highest ideal, never submits to a compromise, whose motto is "All or Nothing". Like Arno Holz, so Hollrieder, after a tenacious struggle for an individual, most subtle form of expression, finally reaches the equation of technique and content, the proportionate valuation of things. Like the picture in the drama, so the drama itself is the masterpiece of Holz-Hollrieder. Both are still dissatisfied; both see an ideal still higher before them in the distance. This strong infusion from the poet's own blood makes Hollrieder a genuine artist. In S a p p h o as well as in T a s s o we meet with sensitive m e n: we have no opportunity to judge of the heroine's or hero's creative talent. Hollrieder i s a creator. His artistic character has been visualized directly and convincingly. His humble respect for nature, his proud self-consciousness in comparison with inferior artists, his fiery temperament, his love of life in contrast with his seclusion from the world: these specifically artistic qualities in him we are made to experience; they are not merely related. This most "subjective" of Holz's characters is entirely objective because it is absolutely natural. Likewise the rest of the d r a - m a t i s p e r s o n a e. Isolated from their author, they are insolubly connected with one another. They form a group, an organism, a microcosm where the least movement of an individual member is transmitted to the entirety, where the pulse of common life continually vibrates through all individual phenomena. The interchange of cause and effect is perfect. The motivation is faultless; the dramatic structure of the greatest possible simplicity and consistency.

The original guilt is nothing accidental as in the case of O e d i p u s or B r i d e o f M e s s i n a. It is neither an unconvincing construction, as in Hebbel's M a r i a M a g - d a l e n e, nor a problematical hypothesis, as in G h o s t s,

but, as in R o s m e r s h o l m, the necessary consequence
of a given combination of characters and situations. The
guilt is as gigantic, as horrible as can be imagined in the
life of man, and yet not beyond our sympathy. Neither
Beatrice nor Lipsius are criminals whom we indifferently
leave to their doom. Relying solely upon his deep knowledge of human nature, the poet succeeds in making us
bow low to a fate which might have overpowered us under
similar conditions. Who dares cast a stone at the unfortunate? With fear and pity we stand, not only before the
sin of these individuals, but also before the abysses of life
as such.

Beatrice has the desire for atonement. Roused by
her sin from the turmoil of blind instincts to full consciousness, she seeks punishment and redemption in death.
Rescued against her will, she strives for purification by the
hard school of life. She atones by renouncing the joys of
the world. The more completely she subdues the demon in
her, the more her feeling of responsibility recedes, —
the more exclusively and severely she condemns her father.
At last he alone seems guilty. He has poisoned her very
life, has blocked her way to the bliss of pure love the value
of which was revealed to her when it was too late. For a
decade she remains in the obscurity of an assumed name,
making, by her extraordinary energy, an externally brilliant
career in foreign countries. Yet her triumphs on the
stage are a disgustingly hollow masquerade to her. Life
has no meaning to her. Only one beautiful sentiment, one

longing, like a hidden spring, feeds her soul: her rescuer
was not a brute like the others.

Her mental torpidity gives way. Life's great joy is
luring. What is holy and good in her begins to bloom.
Hollrieder is the true, strong man destined for her, the
most womanly woman. Boundless bliss would be hers, if
it were not for the past. He is pure. She is disgraced.
Since she loves him, she forces herself to renounce. It
would have lightened her struggle, if she had torn herself
away at once from him whom she found again unexpectedly.
But to serve him she stays near him for months. Her
presence revives his self-confidence weaving, at the same
time, threads from one to the other, the conjunctive power
of which it becomes harder and harder to resist. And yet
she gains the great victory over her heart, when the picture
is finished, when the bitter-sweet period of distant near-
ness comes to an end.

It is not her fault, if Hollrieder crosses her path at
the moment when she is about to depart from him by
departing from his work, which is on exhibition in a public
building. Having saved him for his art, she now can give
him back to life after he has again relapsed into despon-
dency. Purified by her unselfish love for Hollrieder, she
has freed herself from the past. Whatever has happened,
now she gives more than she receives. She has earned a
claim upon the artist; now she offers herself as a sacrifice
to the man who is nothing without her. She knows: an
hour of sublime enjoyment of life may carry him up to the
light for ever. She will soon sink back into darkness her-

self. Events are mightier than she. She must despair of being even worth so much as to enrich the lives of others at the expense of her own self. Amidst new and cruel struggles she resigns again to be lured back to hope for a last time.

The secret has been disclosed, and the impossible happens: Hollrieder does not give her up. Slowly confidence and faith return into her soul. Hollrieder is strong. He does not take her for what she was in the past but for what she actually is now, after all her bitter experiences. He rewards her service to his art and the service she was ready to do for him as a man. Her guilt is redeemed. The past has been buried. A new being, she begins a new life. She becomes the wife of the man she loves.

And now destruction breaks in upon her, suddenly, irresistibly, completely. Yet, out of the ruins of her happiness she rises inwardly victorious. Step by step she ascends to ever greater purity. Her love grows more and more spiritual, more and more unselfish. Now she ultimately casts off the cravings of her senses. Voluntarily she takes her father's guilt upon herself in order to liberate her husband entirely, in order to save him for both art and life. Her husband having despaired of her and all love, she must prove to him that true love is not yet extinct, that her own love has been the true one. In a higher sense than Hollrieder once saved her life, she is now the saviour of his soul. Death for him is her last, her only undisturbed joy.

Beatrice is far from being an angel-like martyr. She

does not throw life away as a toy. The road to the liberating deed is hard and steep. No pain, no humiliation is spared her. She must overcome a final, cruelly deceptive revival of hope, before death becomes the friend in whose arms she finds peace.

Only a great poet, a consummate artist, was able to create this magnificent woman, this heroine in life, suffering, and death. Impelled by the glow of passion, extravagant in love and hatred, awful and fascinating, repulsive and pitiable, unfathomable and transparent, a most complex character, unified by her great longing, ennobled by her devotion and her will for purity, true nature, a genuine woman through and through — Beatrice is a creation of permanence.

Her fate is the tragedy of the time. The question as to the valuation of character by individuality or association has here been given the most acute form. The poet answers in the negative, because the absoluteness of the individual is a phantom, because the influence of past relations never ceases to be a force. While such pessimism is open to doubt, the chaste reserve in the representation of most delicate conditions deserves unlimited praise.

Hollrieder is Beatrice's worthy counterpart. They belong together by elective affinity. She finds in him the noble spirituality for which she strives; he finds in her the noble sensuality which the artist needs. All that the lonely, ever-dissatisfied artist yearns for he sees realized in Beatrice: beauty and magnanimity combined, life itself in its

highest bloom. He meets her when he is about to give
up his long struggle for his ideal. All or nothing was his
motto. Despairingly he begins to believe that he has
attained nothing, that he will attain nothing. Life having
no more charm for him, his art fails. Beatrice's very appearance revives his energy. She is the woman for whom
he renounced the enjoyment of life, for whom he became
a misogynist, because she, the only one, seemed lost to
him. Now she has returned as if by miracle — and is not
his entirely. Between her and him there is a shadow, a
spectre whose terror increases, the more bravely, the more
tenaciously he fights it. He is strong enough to forget a
past guilt, if only Beatrice will be entirely his in the future.
That he cannot believe. His love, at first being primarily
sensual, develops, as with Beatrice, to ever deeper spirituality. The selfish jealousy of the senses which controls
Hebbel's Herodes to the last, in Hollrieder is hightened to
the desire for the exclusiveness of a perfect harmony of
souls. All or nothing, in life as in art.

So Beatrice, with greater justification than Herodes and Mariamne, might be called the tragedy
of soulful sensitiveness. The fight against the past, nearly
won, is lost through distrust in the future. This distrust
has its roots in the very basis of Hollrieder's character as
a man and an artist, in his supreme instinct for totality.
Inexorably severe with himself, he must destroy all that
seems imperfect, incomplete, about him. What he loses is
the full realization of happiness. What he gains is the
purity of reminiscence, the belief in human nature. If he

can bear the grief at Beatrice's death, he will recover as
an artist, and her sacrifice was not in vain.

B e a t r i c e is tragic in the highest possible degree.
In decades no German dramatist conceived more deeply,
visualized more convincingly the tragedy of existence as
such, the tragedy of the idiosyncracy of the individual.
While all characters are most intimately connected with
one another by circumstances, they are, at the same time,
isolated from one another by a mysterious something, an
ultimate power, indefinable, impenetrable. This magnetic
force, the individual's atmospere which attracts and repels,
has never before been expressed to more intensive effect
through the medium of language.

III.

"The greatest lyrical genius" of the generation surprised his contemporaries, at the beginning of the nineties,
by the sporadic publication of poems the form of which
was the extreme contrast to the sonorous rimes and
smooth strophes of T h e B o o k o f t h e T i m e. They
were little things of a peculiar pregnancy and scarcity of
expression, seemingly artless exclamations, primitive and
childlike stammerings compared to the brilliant rhetoric
of the former. The critics called them telegram-lyrics and
would certainly have applied the phrase "barbaric yawp",
if Whitman had then been known as well as he is now.
The poems did not fit into any of the traditional filing-

cases of literature. So only a few connoisseurs priced them at their intrinsic value.

In Harden's Z u k u n f t (April 30th, 1898), in a pamphlet R e v o l u t i o n o f L y r i c s (1899) Arno Holz gave the theory, in the two booklets P h a n t a s u s simultaneously the first collection of his new poetry. The theory is about as follows.: novel and drama, after a long imitative period, at last found their way back again to nature; only the lyric did not. Wherever an attempt was made in this direction, the result were monstrosities such as Whitman's who destroyed the old forms without finding a new one. The lyrical revolution of 1885 was illusory. For the verses of "The Youngest Germans" did not, as to their inner structure, differ from those of Goethe, as the verses of Goethe had not been different from those of the middle ages. As far back as we can trace lyric art: its form was based upon the principle of striving for a certain music through words, for a rhythm which is not only a means toward an end but also an end in itself.

This tendency gradually gave rise to all traditional forms of lyrics without having anything to do with the nature of this art. None of the traditional forms left to the words their essential values: being originally means of expression and decoration at the same time, the forms again and again petrified to mere decorations, decayed, and were stored up in the museum of poetics. As in the case of novel and drama the goal must be: a pure form of expression which, originating from the respective content, develops with the respective complexes of thought and feeling;

that is to say: a lyric art which refrains from any musical
effect by words as an end in itself and which, as regards its
form, is based solely upon a rhythm existing only by what
it strives to express.

Rime and strophe have done good service in their
time. But they are no longer able to adequately express
the infinite diversity of modern life. Nor are the various
phases of socalled "Free Rhythm" (Klopstock, Goethe,
Heine, Whitman, etc.) equal to this task. Free Rhythm,
too, is contaminated with that rhetorical pseudopathos that
robs the words of their intrinsic values. It is, however, the
very essence of the new form to leave to every word its
own individual value. The aim is, therefore, not a free
rhythm but a natural, a necessary, an immanent rhythm:
an absolutely pure form of expression, as far as possible
remote from ulterior, merely communicative purposes,
from rhetorical effects. The words must neither be over-
valued nor undervalued. "Express what you feel directly
as you feel it, and you have the natural rhythm. You
grasp it, grasping the things. It is immanent in all phenomena." Rime, strophe, parallelism, alliteration, asso-
nance, are accessories which the poet may use when they
offer themselves naturally, not, however, for external
decoration.

This "immanent" rhythm grows out of the content
ever anew, as though nothing of the kind had been written
before. It differs from prose (which it necessarily resembles on the printed page) for the reason that it is not a
syntactic scheme for the purpose of communication of

ideas but a concrete visualization of esthetic experiences. Although this rhythm does not intentionally attempt to produce musical effects, it is not unmusical. On the contrary: it being entirely free from conventional limitations and ornamental superficialities, its cadence is the very essence of the musical qualities of the subject-matter. It stands in the same relation to the comparatively monotonous flow of strophic poetry as Richard Strauss's differentiated orchestration to that of previous centuries. Its nature being the greatest possible directness, substantiality, and harmonious diversity, it requires a mastery of language combined with a power of condensation such as only the greatest poets possess. On the other hand, its boundless versatility opens the whole world of human perception to lyrical representation.

Perhaps Arno Holz was wrong in prophesying for his new technique a predominance, in the future, over the conventional forms. Perhaps there will always be innumerable lyric experiences for which rime and strophe constitute the "immanent rhythm", as e. g. in the case of Goethe's Über allen Gipfeln. So much any unbiased critic will have to admit, that true poetry is independent of any convention of form, and that Arno Holz himself, by means of his new technique, created poems of unsurpassed beauty and of a character quite their own.

Phantasus and later additions that appeared in the Munich Jugend and in Deutsche Lyrik der Neuzeit display an amazingly great variety of subjects. The poet's horizon extends from naïve child's talk

to the obscurity of world-riddles, from modern metropolitan to exotic oriental motifs. A classification is impossible. However, some of the more important groups might
be mentioned: the longings, fulfillments, and sorrows of
love; memories of childhood and home, family-scenes;
communion with nature; landscape-grotesques in Böcklin's
style; glimpses into past ages and foreign countries; fancies, dream-visions, philosophical meditations.

Since nearly one fourth of the whole number are
devoted to child-life, Arno Holz deserves a place of honor
besides the best of family poets like Rückert, Dehmel, or
Stevenson. But, while he does justice to the delicate grace,
the roguish candor, the unsophisticated aspirations of pure
youth, he identifies himself as successfully with the gallan-
tries of the man of the world. The little boy who reaches
for every sun-beam and every butterfly, who has forget-
me-not-eyes and loves Ludwig Richter is alive in him side
by side with the modern European who knows the lights
and shadows of society, high and low.

Holz has as pronounced a talent for the effects of contrast as Heine, but differs from him in looking upon the
polarity of life from the serious humorist's point of view.
His imagination, instead of dissociating connected phenomena, tends toward associating the seemingly disconnected.
He never arbitrarily annihilates a sentiment once called
forth as Heine did with his cynic application of romantic
irony. He comprises within a few lines wide expanses of
time and space. His is the great art of reflecting a world
in a miniature mirror. Without ever posing as a cosmic

11*

poet like Whitman, he feels a cosmos in his heart. And
he gives shape to his cosmic feelings with the graceful
ease, with the serene naïveté of a genius who is one with
nature.

A keen thinker, he is aware of the world's eternal
secrets without ever losing himself in vague mysticism.
As honest as Liliencron, he renounces the hope for final
perceptions in this life. The old, fearful question of
Whence and Whither he rejects with humble resignation.
The life of man is a nothing, a fleeting cloud of smoke, a
rain-drop, the buzzing song of the lamp in the dead of
night. Permanent is only the grandeur and glory of
Nature whose inexhaustible wealth puts the rich to shame
and makes life worth living to the poor. Consoling as such
thoughts are, the poet is not spared times of utter despair.
Periods of modest contentment are interupted by embittered accusations and bold defiance of the Creator's incon-
ceivable wisdom.

Holz, for Germany the founder of genuine naturalism,
is at the same time a master of symbolism. Dehmel
nowhere expressed more concretely the mysterious ardor
of erotic passion, than Holz did in his S a l o m e - poem.
Mombert never penetrated more deeply into the dark
secrets of the terrors of night, than Holz did in his dream-
visions. Neither a hundred years ago nor in our own day
did the infinite, abstract, insatiable longing of lonely souls
find more glowing colors, more ringing sounds than Holz's
R o t e R o s e n, I n g r a u e s G r ü n, Ü b e r d i e W e l t
h i n. Many a romanticist fails as an artist. Holz's plastic
power is always equal to its aim. He is a classic. To an

abundance of life he gives the most concentrated form. Whatever his experiences are: their expression is clear, concrete, chaste. He is the strongest artist among the moderns. This he proved unmistakably when, for an interlude, he met conventional poetry on its own ground in the lyric satire T h e T i n - S h o p (B l e c h s c h m i e d e) and in the humorous revival of the lyrics of the baroque-period D a f n i s.

Within three generations Germany has had no lyric poet who may boast of such a variety of forms and motifs, who equally commands the tone of delicate grace and fiery passion, who so perfectly combines the charms of humor with ethical depth. And this same poet is no less great as a dramatist. He not only knows how to project himself; he projects his fellow-men as well and with the same degree of force: two faculties usually excluding each other. And in the drama, too, the extent of his art is unlimited. It reaches from exhilarating comedy to overwhelming trage-dy. And one more gift is peculiar to this dramatic lyricist or lyrical dramatist: he is capable of abstract thinking. To the latter gift is due his art-law which shows the way to a real science of art. This strange combination that enabled him to carry out one of the most fruitful known reforms in literature, gives him the place of a perfectly unique pheno-menon. If he had been favored by fate as he was hindered, if another twenty years of undisturbed activity had been granted to him, who knows but that Arno Holz would rank among the very greatest geniuses of literature? He is the Kleist of our time.

VI.

Heinrich Mann

————

The first and prevailing impression of Heinrich Mann's writings is that of an unbridled and disgusting sensuality which appears in the garb of an overheated, romantically embellished pathos. The reader is constantly reminded of Heine's A r d i n g h e l l o , of Tieck's W i l - l i a m   L o v e l l, of Friedrich Schlegel's L u c i n d e , of Gabriele D'Annunzio. It is the ennervating atmosphere of a society which, without vital aims, without the necessity of work, leads a life, not "beyond good and evil" but in the very midst of vice; a society which, remote from the brisk air-currents of progressive humanity, enclosed within a dream-world of voluptuous fancies, knows of only one struggle: the paralizing vacillation between the affectations of an over-refined culture and barbaric lusts.

And yet an author should be studied outside his own country who, by critics of note, is declared the creator of the modern German novel; who, by esthetically sensitive readers, is revered as one of the foremost geniuses of our time; who indeed, in his best writings, displays an extra-ordinary talent, and who, like Wieland after his lascivious period, may be destined to produce some great work of permanent value in the future.

Born in 1871 as the son of a North German merchant and a lady of Southern descent, educated in the environment of the Lübeck patricians, Heinrich Mann first attracted attention in 1897 with a small volume of short stories the style of which showed the influence of Paul Heyse and Theodor Storm, while its dreamy suggestiveness recalled older romanticists like Eichendorff. — The best of these stories T h e   W o n d r o u s   (D a s   W u n d e r b a r e) the author surpassed later in the mastery of technique but not in its uniformly enrapturing poetry. "The wondrous" is a perfectly spiritualized love, a singular experience in the life of a man of affairs, an experience so free from all earthly disturbances, so heavenly that it remains for ever the resting place of his aspirations, the paradise of his dreams. This ideal which he keeps unmarred by any contact with the world, which represents the sanctuary of his soul, is the power that lifts him, the seemingly prosaic business man, up above the artists, the professional wardens of beauty. For them who are compelled to live in close contact with the ideal so that they may give it shape in their works, for them the ideal is deprived of its most peculiar charm — "the wondrous". This story is a lyric poem, a song of grief and longing and renunciation, but of a renunciation that makes man wise and efficient in the struggle for the attainable.

There followed — an almost incredible contrast — a series of erotic novels and stories that shared, to a deplorable degree, the superficial sensationalism of Sudermann's S o n g   o f   S o n g s. It is only in his very latest works

that Heinrich Mann showed himself once more worthy of
serious attention, even if he extended the range of his
subjects but little, preserving his preference for erotic
motives. The titles of his recent books are: The Bad
(Die Bösen), The Heart (Das Herz), two collec-
tions of short stories, and The Small Town (Die
kleine Stadt), a novel. A one-act play published this
year, 1911, is too frivolous to deserve consideration. One
of the two stories in The Bad is Branzilla, the other
The Tyrant. "Branzilla" is a great Italian singer who
makes her art the moloch of her life, to whom she sacri-
fices the happiness of others and her own soul.

This story is composed in a technique that Heinrich
Mann had gradually acquired in former works of his,
going back partly to Flaubert, partly to Holz-Schlaf's
Papa Hamlet. The action rests entirely upon the
dialog. The narration, limited to the smallest possible
space, produces the effect of stage-directions. Separate
periods of time are, in the manner of scenes, put together
without direct connections so as to make the impression
of perspective continuity. Since the narrating transitions
are lacking and the changes of time and space are indi-
cated in the dialog only, the author's personality being
entirely eliminated, the reader's imagination is forced to a
most intense co-operation. He has, therefore, at the end
an image in his mind of all happenings as plastic, as if he
had been watching a theatrical performance. Branzilla, a sketch of a few pages, comprises a long life. In
spite of its external brevity there is the illusion of length,

because the most essential features of the heroine's life are skilfully selected and grouped. However, this "dramatic" technique does not necessarily lead up to a real drama. B r a n z i l l a gives a stationary character in different situations and illuminations, while there is no inner conflict caused by antagonistic will-impulses. Branzilla's rigid egotism is scarcely ever stirred by a sympathetic feeling. Still it would be erroneous to think that the story itself is cold. There is enough of passion and suffering — only it is not rhetorically expressed. Feeling breaks forth here and there like flashes of lightning from a dark sky.

Similar remarks may be made concerning T h e T y r a n t. Here "the bad one", a young prince, the ruler of an Italian city, succeeds in overcoming his love for a beautiful woman who, as the avenger of her family, has come to him, as Judith came to Holofornes, in order to entice and kill him. With her, love conquers hatred; with the tyrant the opposite takes place. To the woman's submissive confidence which he diabolically incites, he responds by inflicting capital punishment upon her. With great force, audacity, and psychological subtlety "the eternal contest between the sexes", as Hebbel put it, has been treated in this story. The whole of it is an ingenious, if indeed satanic, play with the noblest and purest sentiments of the human heart, a gloomy, yet magnificent, picture of the Italian Renaissance when mankind pendulated between the lofty ideal of the superman and the savage ferocity of beasts of prey.

The collection T h e H e a r t is of uneven value. Beside

a trivial piece of citizen-life and a balladesque tale of
jealousy in Paul Heyse's style, beside two romantic stories
suggesting the bizarre method of Hoffmann, there is a
masterpiece of perfect originality: T h e I n n o c e n t
O n e (D i e U n s c h u l d i g e). A celebrated physician
has been murdered in his own house. Circumstances cast
a strong suspicion upon his young wife. She is imprisoned
for a year, while her trial is going on. A lawyer whom she
secretely loved, before the murder happened, brings about
her acquittal. The criminal remains unknown. After the
lapse of some time the woman is married to her attorney.
— It is the evening of their wedding day. The horrors of
the past events, the murder, the terrible suspense in prison,
the long trial, press upon the woman's soul. She cannot
believe in her future without having finally tested the character of him who is now her husband. Was she "not
guilty" indeed? Does she know herself after the thousand-
fold torture of public exposure, of crossquestionings, of
loneliness in her cell? Her own nurse considers her
guilty — and stays with her as faithful as ever. Her husband must love her, even if she is guilty. For if she is, she
committed the deed, because she loved him. If he does
not love her in spite of her guilt, he does not possess that
all-compelling passion for her which triumphs over all
conventions, which fuses body and soul into one, that love
for which she has always been craving, and which she has
in store for her liberator. The moment of decision arrives.
When her husband enters the bridal chamber, she places
the fearful dilemma before him. In an ecstasy of contra-

dictory feelings, accusing herself, she brings forward once
more all the causes for suspicion that his art had removed;
she raises new points, showing herself a shrewder prose-
cutor, than he had been a defender. And he succumbs.
Believing her guilty, he shrinks back from her shudderingly.
Then he perceives that he was wrong, and repents. It is
too late for that grand, boundless love. They must
acquiesce in a compromise. He pleads: "We can love each
other still, can we not?" She replies: "Yes: as human
beings love each other. They confide in each other to a
certain degree; they understand each other by means of
indulgence; they are one on condition."

While this story is written in the style of B r a n -
z i l l a , another in the same volume is of an older date and
technique: T h e A c t r e s s (D i e S c h a u s p i e l e r i n).
This contains an analysis of the author's own character,
his two principal traits being represented by the heroine
and her counterpart Mr. Rothaus. The actress longs for
a full enjoyment of life through the happiness of love.
Mr. Rothaus, the refined and sensitive man, is condemned
to asceticism chiefly by his esthetic delicacy. At the
same time he too longs for the naive joys of existence and
is bound to the actress by this very longing, until he tears
himself away to live on in solitude. The actress again,
who as a human being would break down under her
disappointment, finds consolation in her art. She recognizes that never, even in the hours of most intense suffering, her misery had perfect control of her. Even then
she was always both the suffering woman and the creative

artist who involuntarily objectivated her own subjective experiences. This ability of self-projection is her salvation: "There was in her a stage upon which, a second time and in smaller proportions, she acted her own experiences until she had played herself tired . . . Presenting her sufferings to herself, she forgot that she suffered; forgot it more and more."

The same discrepancy of feeling is the subject of an earlier story Pippo Spano where the author portrays both himself and D'Annunzio in the same character. His self-scrutiny is as keen and icy as Strindberg's, when he confesses to a bewildering mixture of genuine sentiment and studied pose, of real self-control and morbid ambition which, instead of rating men and things according to their original and individual values, views them exclusively as material for "artistic" purposes. Therefore, unable to lose himself entirely in another person, the artist is forever alone. Heinrich Mann is all the more conscious of this solitude as his inner disunion is intensified by his descent. Both as an artist and as a man he stands Between Races which title he gave one of his novels. Southern sensuousness and Northern idealism in him are in permanent conflict.

So his latest novel The Small Town (Die kleine Stadt) again represents the struggle between life and asceticism. The chief motives of his earlier works are all united here, as Felix Stoessinger has pointed out: the artist who keeps himself apart from life, and his contrast, the man who enjoys life; the egotistically ambitious

woman of Branzilla's type, and the woman who throws herself away. "The small town" is somewhere in Italy. A
progressive party of citizens has, for a season, engaged an
operatic company against the protest of a conservative
minority under the leadership of the priest. The appearance of the artists has the effect of Circe's magic wand.
The light morals of the guests, together with the power
of their music, transform the residence of respectable
citizens into a temple of Venus Vulgata. It is perhaps the
greatest merit of the book to make the readers feel how
the mellow, enticing music spreads from the opera-house
over the whole community, gradually reaching and influenc-
ing all inhabitants, finally even ringing in the ears of the
hostile priest while he prays. The grotesque conclusion
is this, that through a fair sinner a reconciliation is effected between the opponents. The artists leave the place.
The priest, however, has himself experienced the mysterious power of life and love. He will be more tolerant
in the future. Since he is not allowed to love one individual, he gives his heart to mankind. Fate demands one
victim: a young couple whose blind passion of love reminds
one of Romeo and Juliet, are ruined by envious gossip.

Various critics praised this novel in the most extravagant terms, one going so far as to declare it the greatest
literary accomplishment since Flaubert. Indeed, there is
a technical skill, a control of the linguistic means of expression which can hardly be surpassed. The language is so
completely adapted to the Italian environment as to make

the impression of a masterly translation from that tongue. It is full of metallic sonority, full of melody and rhythm, reflecting, as it were, Italy's blue sky and brilliant colors. There are few works in German literature like this: young Heyse's best stories and K. F. Meyer's T h e T e m p t a - t i o n o f P e s c a r a and T h e M o n k ' s W e d d i n g. But otherwise the technique, however well it is handled, seems problematical. What in the short story leads to dramatic scenes, here leads to chaos. Dialog replaces narration to such an extent as to make it often impossible to understand the buzz of voices. Too much happens before our very eyes. The novel knows of no presuppositions or secondary motives that might be disposed of by means of brief narration. We are forced to ascend all stairs, to count all windows, to know all costumes, and all gossip. The grandiose effect of concentration in B r a n z i l l a is here given up for a minute enumeration of details which, as with Zola, distract our attention from essentials. The short stories are distinguished by their harmonious propor- tions; here everything is disproportionate, exaggerated, confusing.

Having finished the book, we think that we are very familiar with "the small town". But life in this town is badly monotonous and quite unreal. Its people are mere shadows appearing only in a single and strangely spectral relation to life. Such onesidedness, the emphasis being laid upon one remarkable character-trait or one remarkable event, is the nature of the short story; it decomposes the novel. In his next novel Heinrich Mann should heed Goethe's warning as to the use of dialog: he should narrate, not act it. He would do better still, if he cultivated his proper field, the dramatic short story. There he can serve as a model of form. Beyond this, his influence does not reach; nor is it desirable that it should.

Art has no duration, if it does not take its inspiration from life directly, instead of from an arbitrary play with life or from a contemptuous view of it. What have Oscar Wilde's flowery phrases to say to posterity? Heinrich Mann makes one of his self-portraits say: "The tenor of my life is barrenness, as though nothing ever had happened." And another: "He loved things chiefly for their after-taste, the love of women only for the bitter solitude following, happiness, if at all, for the choking yearning which it leaves in one's throat." In this he represents the decadent phase of romanticism. Indeed, since, as a young man, he experienced the beautiful "wonder" in which he believed, nothing happened to him to create a harmonious impression. His world is the sham of the theater, the artist with half-true feelings, the cynical epicurean. He knows of no pure woman, no unselfish man, no pure deed, not even a pure child. From the mystic faith of Novalis that had given him strength, he drifted to Friedrich Schlegel's irony, developing it to anarchic scepticism. What Nietzsche said of Flaubert is true of Heinrich Mann: it is not the love of life but the hatred of life that makes him write.

In a fine analytical study of Flaubert's relation to

George Sand (perhaps his best work) Mann himself ascribes
to his great master a fervid love of life which over-sensiti-
veness forbade him to admit. If his own apparent hatred
is such a love in disguise, he is guilty of the same fatal
deception which is Heine's great sin, a deception more
pernicious than the most radical negation.

VII.

Thomas Mann

———

Brought up in the same environment as his elder brother, Thomas Mann (born in 1875) faced the same problems. In him, too, North and South, spiritualism and materialism are in conflict with each other. And, besides being placed in the equivocal position between two races, he too, through his creative instinct, feels isolated from the masses, experiences the cold loneliness of the observing artist whose human heart yearns for a naive intercourse with his fellowmen. He knows of the romantic quest for a land of beauty where all dreams are fulfilled. He knows of the imaginative mind's paralyzing disappointment, seeing reality always remain behind his expectations.

In his very first collection of short stories Little M r. F r i e d e m a n n (D e r k l e i n e H e r r F r i e d e - m a n n, 1898), he makes such disharmonious sentiments his theme. D i s a p p o i n t m e n t (E n t t ä u s c h u n g) is a globe-trotter's confession of his t a e d i u m v i t a e. T h e C l o w n (D e r B a j a z z o) represents a fantastic man, who, half an artist, half an amateur, has many talents for the amusement of others, without being strong enough to devote himself wholly to art or wholly to practical life. The consequence is his ultimate failure in everything. Too late he finds the truth that there is only one misfortune in life: the lack of self-confidence. All the misery of the world is of some positive value; inner disunion is absolutely destructive. — On the basis of such knowledge the author shows in other stories what manly heroism and will-power may accomplish. In his own soul he overcomes the fatal discrepancies and finds the magic key to the eternal treasures of life.

While there is a pronounced sense of the ironical and even grotesque in him, he never yields to it entirely. Always superior is his love which enables him to win our sympathy even for the ridiculous and absurd. In contrast with his brother, Thomas Mann possesses humor: not that intrusive, self-conscious, baroque and somewhat plebeian humor of Dickens with whom he is frequently compared, but the reserved, fine, polished humor of a spiritual aristocrat who can love men and things even when they are below him.

Such sympathetic, yet distant, humor gives the tragic story of Little Mr. Friedemann its peculiar charm which established the young author's fame. A wealthy merchant, shut out from the enjoyment of life by physical deformity, step by step acquires the modest happiness of resignation. Suddenly his peace breaks down, when he is seized with an irresistible passion for a beautiful and coquettish woman. Cast off by her like a toy, he dies, alone and pitiable as he had lived.

A later collection Tristan (1903) again treats of the relation of the negative and affirmative of life and of the artist's attitude toward the objects of his observation. One of the stories is autobiographical in substance: Tonio

K r ö g e r. It reads like a counterpart to Heinrich Mann's
T h e W o n d r o u s , more like a poem in prose than an
epic narration; and it is full of romantic longing. But here
the wondrous is not an e x o t i c dream-land. The poet
sees his own native province in the glorifying light of
reminiscence. He abhors the dark-eyed Southerness with
their animal passions. He loves his home-world, the life
of the pure, the cheerful, the light-faced, the happy, the
amiable, the average people — a life which he can never
fully share. For their language is not his. They accomplish practical things and enjoy life at the same time. He is
their inferior as a fellow-man, their superior as an artist.
So he resigns himself to his bitter-sweet loneliness, to his
distant love "in which there is contained some longing and
some melancholic envy, and a little bit of contempt, and
an entire, chaste bliss".

This motif is also touched upon in the title-story
T r i s t a n , the irony here being more strongly accentuat-
ed. However, both works are far more than self-confes-
sions. Both reveal a rare faculty of representing man and
nature in their correlation. Both are symptomatic as
regards their technique. In a highly original manner
similar or contrasting situations are repeated and in their
effect intensified by repetition. That is to say: the rhythmical sequences of words that expressed the essence of the
first situation are here and there taken up again to express
the new situation, simultaneously reminding of the first
one. This is done with the same, apparently unintentional,
graceful easiness which characterizes Richard Wagner's

Leitmotive. Thereby, e. g., youth and mature age of an individual are shown in their unity; the continuity of time is maintained; the principal theme of the whole work, shining forth through all single parts, is brought out at the end with the greatest possible force of concentration. Such a technique is the result of a distinctly musical memory which, combined with the author's plastic power, produces, even in his extensive novels, an astonishing density of composition. As to his musical talent, Mann has given us interpretations of music by words, so exhaustive as to overshadow completely Heine's famous transscription of Paganini's playing.

The subject of the Tristan-stories received its final expression in a splendid renaissance-drama Fiorenza where Lorenzo Medici, the patron of art and lover of beauty, is contrasted with the ascetic priest Girolamo (Savonarola). Neither here nor in his stories — excellent, as they are — does Thomas Mann's genius appear at its very best. The pointedness of the novella proper seems to be more in the line of Heinrich Mann's studied intellectuality. At any rate, the younger brother has made the short story a vehicle of lyrical outbursts so often as to obscure his immense faculty of strict objectivation. It is in the novel that he overcomes the onesidedness of his problems and does justice to the full range of life. He has created, so far, two novels which harmonize romantic profundity of psychology with breadth of vision and realism of representation. They are the most perfect examples of artistic and poetical prose-fiction in modern German literature.

The Buddenbrooks, Decay of a Fa-
mily (1901) has had the singular fate of becoming very
popular in spite of its utter lack of sensationalism. Within
a decade it reached the number of fifty editions. It may
be classed as a modern Debit and Credit standing
higher than Freytag's masterpiece in the same degree as
our sense of style has become more refined, and as the
author's temperament is more genuinely poetic than
Freytag's. The work gives the history of four generations
of a Lübeck merchant-family.

Johann Buddenbrook Senior and his wife Antoinette,
are children of the eighteenth century. They have, through
the storms of the Napoleonic wars, kept up the gentle
serenity, the amiable frivolity of rationalism, the naively
selfish sense for the pleasures of existence. The firm is
prosperous. The family belongs to the group of prominent
patricians, enjoying an unquestioned and general esteem.
It is the "good old time" when the success of a business
house still depended upon the modest and substantial
merits of industry and efficiency, when speculation was
scorned as ignoble, when the employers were the patriarchical guardians of their employées.

Johann Buddenbrook, Junior is of a more stern and
sober nature than his father. In his religion he has returned
from rationalism to dogmatic protestantism. As a businessman he continues the traditions of the firm. He is
economical and conservative in his transactions, working
along with tenacious application. Business is normal, but
there is no expansion. Outside the house of Buddenbrook

a new spirit develops. Social conditions approach a revolution. More forceful business methods come into vogue.
Jewish capital and speculative enterprise compete successfully with the solidity and dignity of the native patricians.
But the reputation of the firm is still intact. Personally
Consul Buddenbrook achieves the triumph of his life,
when, in the turbulent year of revolutions, 1848, by his
presence of mind and by the weight of his name he brings
the excited population to order. Private misfortune coun-
teracts such gain. His daughter Antonie is, against her
inclination, married to a man who turns out to be a swin-
dler. Her dowry is wasted. Her divorce is a scandal.

Consul Buddenbrook's son and successor has a more
modern view of life. A brilliant personality, energetic,
intelligent, circumspect, he rapidly wins the admiration of
his fellow-citizens, when, as a young man, he has become
the head of the firm. Business increases again. A happy
marriage with a wealthy heiress, Gerda, adds new splendor
to his house. He has a son. He is elected Senator of his
republican city. He builds him a magnificent residence.
And when the firm celebrates its one hundredth anniver-
sary, it seems to be in greater prosperity than ever before.
But Thomas himself is haunted by the feeling that the
climax of external success is the beginning of the end.
He is right. A second, equally unhappy, marriage of Antonie and the loss of the dowry and heritage of a younger
sister weaken both the reputation of the family and the
credit of the firm. Thomas is induced to speculate for
once : it is a failure. Now he becomes rigidly conservative.

The advantageous opportunities of the year 1871 with its abundance of money he allows to pass by unused. He gets tired, restless, nervous.

Thomas's son, Hanno, is a sickly and dreamy boy. While he inherited from his mother a strong musical talent, his body is unable to endure the violent emotions of his art. And mother and child are united against husband and father by this art. Thomas becomes o lonely man, suffering intensely from his isolation. Gerda's love seems to be directed to a friend of the house. Now father and son have one thing in common: their sufferings.

Depressed by his sorrows, worn out by an excess of work, Thomas prepares for death. He turns to mysticism and is granted an entrancing revelation of immortality. But, engaged again in the routine of every-day life, he falls back from the heights of inspiration into conventional dogmatism/ without finding peace there. His end comes suddenly and in a most pitiful way: he breaks down in the street. Since Hanno is unfit for the career of a businessman, Thomas in his will has ordered the firm to be dissolved. Hanno dies at an early age. His mother returns to her native city. The name of The Buddenbrooks is no more than the shadow of a powerful race of the past.

When this work appeared, its author was a young man of twenty-six. It has all the virtues of youth, non of its deficiencies. It is mature in thought and technique. The composition is refreshingly simple and straightforward. With a matter-of-fact certainty of touch the difficult task is accomplished of following the history of a merchant-house through half a century without resorting to a mechanical construction, without distracting confusion. There is the ideal concept of "the firm", as in D e b i t a n d C r e d i t, but none of the idealizing abstraction of a commercial providence. We have to do with a thoroughly concrete complex of personal aspirations. "The firm" is the heart of a family with all the fluctuations of life.

Since the last representative of the firm already lives at a time, when its senior head is still enjoying a healthy old age, the connection of human interest is nowhere interrupted by historical reports. To be sure, we are given references to the early history of the Buddenbrooks but in a way directly bearing upon the fate of the characters present. On the whole we are made to live with the family. And it is one of the most admirable features of the novel that time really glides on and on by imperceptible stages. One generation gradually replaces another after having existed together as a seemingly inseperable unit.

The action, unromantic though it be, is never tiresome. Monotony is guarded against, not by sensational episodes, but by an intimate account of the lives of the individual members of the group, all their separate experiences reacting upon the life of the main body. Furthermore, the family appears in close connection with their city and their country. In a wisely limited, yet perfectly sufficient measure the important political, economic, and social events are brought into play: the Napoleonic invasion, the revolutions of 1848, the struggle for Schleswig-Holstein, the Austrian war of 1866, the great year of 1870/71.

As masterly as the composition is the characterization. The problem of heredity, environment, and education is treated in a scientific spirit and with poetic means. What causes the extinction of the Buddenbrooks is not demoralization but an increasing refinement and differentiation of characters. As long as the Buddenbrooks are naively human and not given to philosophizing introspection, as long as they perform their daily duties conscientiously, if prosaically, taking their full share of leisure — so long the success of the firm is assured. — Thomas, by far the most important character in the novel, has inherited his ancestors' business intellect. But a slight artistic talent in his grandfather, with him becomes a strong taste for literature. And in choosing his wife he is determined not only by her wealth but also by her art which, at the end, is largely the cause of disunion. Thomas wishes to be "modern" but is too sensitive to follow modern business methods consistently. He has to struggle against a tendency toward fantastic dreaming. His iron self-control is truly heroic: he wants to do things instead of meditating about things. But this his inner conflict is one of the elements that undermine his strength.

Besides the leaders of the firm there are a great number of other characters, all of them sharply individualized: the large Buddenbrook family itself with its various ramifications, other patricians, common people, army officers, clergymen, school-teachers and their pupils, servants etc.

All in all an imposing wealth of situations, persons, philosophies — mastered by the author at an age, when minor talents only begin to realize life's infinite diversities.

The technique throughout the work is naturalistic, i. e. of that lucidity, directness, objectivity, and manifold unity which is a reflex of true nature. So mature, so excellent in every way is this work that intelligent readers doubted wheter its creator would ever develop beyond it. But there was, indeed, a steady advance. Too genuinely aristocratic and not forced by external conditions to exploit his first successes, Thomas Mann has so far produced comparatively little: n o n m u l t a s e d m u l t u m. He has been striving for still greater perfection of his art. His second novel: H i s R o y a l H i g h n e s s (K ö n i g l i c h e H o h e i t 1908) is superior even to the B u d d e n b r o o k s.

"Known and yet a stranger, he moves about among the people, walks with the crowd, yet, as it were, surrounded by an empty space; goes along lonesome, carrying upon his slender shoulders the burden of his highness." It is His Royal Highness Klaus Heinrich, the heir presumptive of the throne of "Grimmburg", a principality somewhere in Germany. The story is not of the external pomp of a court but of the inner development of a fine young man who, placed in an exalted position by Providence, fights a long struggle in order that he may have a share of the world. From the very beginning of his life, through all the years of his childhood, he is never allowed to be quite himself nor to abandon himself entirely to others. Self-control, dignity, is the one lesson he has to

learn, the one standard he has to follow always. He is an
indefinable something, a symbol representing an abstract
idea — "the people". He is like an elf who lives a sham-
existence, having no soul to unite him with the real life of
real human beings. As a boy he timidly starts out with
his little sister to discover the unknown about him which
he vaguely divines. But what they find are only deserted
halls of the old castle; and the greatest event for them in
many years is an encounter with an honest shoemaker
who speaks in a natural language, the directness of which
impresses them as both amusing and shocking. Klaus
Heinrich attends a "gymnasium" and spends a year at a
university — for show. For show he is dressed in an officer's uniform and watches a few military exercises. He
makes a journey through Europe so well guarded by his
courier as to be unable to even check a trunk.

After the death of their father, the grand-duke, his
elder brother, being of frail health, leaves all the duties of
representation to him. At public festivities, at dedications
of monuments, in charitable institutions, Klaus Heinrich
"represents" the court. In everything he takes part to a
certain degree, in nothing his whole self is absorbed. For
no one penetrates through the aura of his "Highness". He
as well as his people are enchained in a spell of conventions.
He, the most conspicuous man in the country, is the most
lonely.

At last there enter his sphere two persons not bound
by any convention, independent because of infinite wealth,
isolated from the masses by this wealth, as Klaus Heinrich

by his position: it is the German-American billionair Mr. Spoelmann and his beautiful daughter Imma. The prince and Imma become friends. But the obstacles that separate them are great: the conventions of rank and blood. Greater still is another hindrance. Imma has no confidence in Klaus Heinrich. She is a woman of activity and free resolutions. The prince's sham-life seems uncanny and repulsive to her. The second part of the book is devoted to this conflict and its solution. The difference in rank is bridged over by Spoelmann's wealth that saves the country from bankruptcy. Klaus Heinrich bravely overcomes his personal limitations. He learns how to value men according to their intrinsic worth; he undertakes serious studies for the benefit of his people. Imma's love redeems him and gives him a soul; he liberates Imma from her isolation. They find happiness in a noble love that includes the happiness of their country.

This story, in its symbolical suggestiveness, is intended to approach the character of a fairy-tale. For a long time the rich "uncle from America" has been a motif in German fiction: he comes unexpectedly, when distress is greatest, to make everybody happy with his silver-dollars. This motif here appears in such dimensions as to make it no less poetical than the ancient fairy-tales where kingdoms are rescued and princesses won by foreign adventurers. While modern Germany never had such an experience in reality, it ought to have it according to the author's idea. For then, at last, its ultra-conservatism would be broken, the misery of aristocratic intermarriages and social discrimination relieved. The individual would come to his own. Imma, the fascinating little American lady is a princess in a higher sense than the daughters of native nobility. Thomas Mann employed his whole art in order to raise this character into the realm of the strange, unique, wonderful, and sublime, giving it at the same time the charm of concrete humanity. This is the difference between Mann's fairy-tale and traditional fiction: his men and women are typical, indeed, and symbolical, but not in the sense of abstract haziness. They are typical, because they are so thoroughly human. We live their lives with them, knowing both their virtues and their weaknesses. Still they retain a lustre of sacredness for us like precious jewels which even daily use never deprives of their ideal beauty.

It goes without saying that the crude and absurd elements of popular fairy-tales have been avoided. The power of public opinion and superstitions in regard to certain prophecies is skilfully used to good effect without sacrificing logical causation. On the basis of the given suppositions everything not only can but must come about as it does. With the author's customary foresight the final effects are carefully prepared, the individual motifs, the characters, the environment of court, city, and country, brought into close correlation. No event comes with disturbing forcefulness; no word, no sound is lost; there is tact and grace of expression in every line. The form is as dignified as the plot: noble, pure, classic.

Thomas Mann's consummate art and no less his personal self-command, discretion, and wisdom entitle us to

great expectations for the future. He has not been estrang-
ed from collective life by his consciousness of individual
isolation, by his romantic longing for an ideal. Like Germany's two greatest novelists before him, Goethe and
Keller, he has conquered the disharmony of scepticism by
realizing the redeeming power of social service.